# THE
# CONFIDENT
# CHRISTIAN

# THE
# CONFIDENT
# CHRISTIAN

## by
## Wilbur E. Nelson

Thomas Nelson Publishers
Nashville

Published in Nashville, Tennessee, by Thomas Nelson, Inc., Publishers and distributed in Canada by Lawson Falle, Ltd., Cambridge, Ontario.

Printed in the United States of America.

Old Testament Scripture quotations in this book are from the King James Version of the Bible.

New Testament Scripture quotations in this book are from the New King James Bible-New Testament. Copyright © 1979, Thomas Nelson, Inc., Publishers.

*Library of Congress Cataloging in Publications Data*

Nelson, Wilbur E.
    The confident Christian.

    Includes bibliographical references.
    1. Bible. N.T. Corinthians, 2nd—Meditations.
I. Title.
BS2675.4.N44     1981          227'.307          81–38424
ISBN 0–8407–5777–8                 AACR2

# CONTENTS

# PREFACE

Previous books I have written have made me aware of some of the hazards of being an author. One such pitfall is that life and learning are progressive, while a book "freezes" the product and progress of the moment. Sections may be written when the mind is facile and words flow freely, other parts when thoughts turn fugitive and words recalcitrant. Months after sending a manuscript to a publisher, an author can be faced with pages filled with words he cannot believe he chose and thoughts he may have outgrown. Such may be the case with this book, but still the commitment must be made, the publishing date honored. I offer these chapters with the prayer that they may be useful to those who, like myself, admire the trying, sometimes even tempestuous, wrestling of the apostle Paul with the Corinthians.

Wilbur E. Nelson
November, 1980

# INTRODUCTION

Second Corinthians was obviously written by Paul while enduring a time of deep distress and disappointment. Still concerned with the problems with which he had dealt in his first Corinthian epistle, apparently only partially remedied, Paul also had to face a group of Judaizers new to the Corinthian church. Bearing impressive letters of introduction and commendation, these men formed an alliance with an anti-Paul element in the church, and soon an ugly, insolent collection of charges was made against the apostle. He was accused of being both theologically and morally tainted, unworthy of apostolic authority.

In view of Paul's deep love for the Corinthian church, we can easily understand the anguish this rebellion caused him. He apparently went to Corinth to face his opponents in person but was unable to solve the problem by discussion. It seems that he then returned to Ephesus, which had been his base, and wrote what has been called his "stern letter," probably taken to Corinth by Titus. After some time, during which Paul waited anxiously for news of the letter's effect, Titus brought good news. The rebellion was over, and the church again recognized the apostolic leadership of Paul. Naturally Paul wrote once again to the Corinthian church, expressing his relief and gratitude and, at the same time, defending his character, his apostolic authority, and his message. He even responded to snide comments about his size and appearance.

What the apostle wrote we call Second Corinthians. Actually, Paul may have written several other letters to the Corinthian church, with only two of them appearing in the New Testament. A minority of students believe that three of those

9

letters appear, interpreting 2 Corinthians 10–13 as part of a
separate letter which came, somehow, to be included in this
epistle.

The purpose of these studies is to deal not with the theoreti-
cal problem of other possible epistles, but with what is here, in
the Second Corinthians we know. Biblical scholars and critics
are not the intended audience, but rather those who welcome
practical help in understanding the message of the epistle.

The format is based on the exposition of passages, not single
words, and involves the setting forth of conclusions developed
from prayerful contemplation and responsible research. An
effort has been made to avoid duplicating the work of those fine
scholars whose books make careful distinctions in the meaning
of words, some of which do not really bear upon the meaning of
the passage. These distinctions in word meanings will be pur-
sued here only when they are essential to clarifying the passage.

# 1

## ABOUNDING CONSOLATION
## IN CHRIST

*2 Cor. 1:1–7*
**1** Paul, an apostle of Jesus Christ by the will of God, and Timothy our brother, To the church of God which is at Corinth, with all the saints who are in all Achaia: **2** Grace to you and peace from God our Father and the Lord Jesus Christ.

Paul greeted the Corinthians as "an apostle [one sent ] of Jesus Christ by the will of God . . . ," a description used frequently in his other epistles. Given the challenges to his apostolate by the repudiated Judaizers, though, this reiteration of a standard phrase probably carried more than the usual emphasis and gratitude. The repentant Corinthians had to be reminded that the choice actually never had been theirs; the will of God and not human assignment or ecclesiastical commission had made Paul an apostle. "Timothy our brother" was mentioned along with Paul, not as a coauthor of the epistle but as a beloved friend and partner in Paul's apostolic labors. With his identity established, Paul was then ready to conclude his greeting by invoking upon "the church of God" at Corinth, with all the saints who were in all Achaia, God's "grace and peace," those twin treasures by which the people of God are divinely sustained, energized, and gladdened in heart.

### COMFORT IN SUFFERING

**3** Blessed be the God and Father of our Lord Jesus Christ, the Father of mercies and God of all comfort, **4** who comforts us in all our tribulation, that we may be able to comfort those who are in any trouble, by the comfort with which we ourselves are comforted by God. **5** For as the sufferings of Christ abound in us, so our consolation also abounds by Christ. **6** And if we are afflicted, it is for your consolation and salvation, which is effective for enduring the same sufferings which we also suffer. Or if we are comforted, it is for your consolation and salvation. **7** And our hope for you is steadfast, knowing that as you are partakers of the sufferings, so you also will be of the consolation.

Perhaps no doxology ever written by Paul is more filled with gratitude and relief than is this passage. Suffering had been meted out to Paul since the day of his conversion, and it had come abundantly in the forms of rejection, humiliation, and affliction. Even the threat of death was one Paul knew well. But now, having valiantly and faithfully "borne the toil and endured the pain," he blessed the God who "comforts us in all our tribulation."

For the verb of support and help used throughout this passage, a minority of scholars prefer the translation "encourage" rather than "comfort." Whichever word is chosen must imply more than mere soothing or sympathy, so if "comfort" is preferred, its meaning must be broadened beyond its modern usage. James Hastings points out, for instance, that one common archaic use of the verb "to comfort" was simply "to communicate strength."* Comfort and fortitude have the same root in common; the intent of God is not merely to bring solace but also strength.

## AN IMPORTANT CHRISTIAN PRINCIPLE

The comfort we receive from God is bestowed not for our benefit only, but "that we may be able to comfort those who are

---

*James Hastings, ed., *The Great Texts of the Bible: II Corinthians/Galatians* (Edinburgh, Scotland: Scribners, 1912), p. 5.

in any trouble." Here Paul propounded a lofty, but often overlooked, Christian principle. The troubles we endure, whatever effect they have on us, are beneficial because they help us to accept our need of divine intervention and deliverance. Driven to seek God's help, we are also drawn by His promises: "Call upon me in the day of trouble; I will deliver Thee . . ." (Ps. 50:15). Our heavenly Father honors such promises and does deliver us—but by a deliverance that should not be selfishly hoarded. It is given to us not only as evidence of God's love and care but also as a benefit to be shared with others who are still troubled, burdened, and afflicted. God deals with us with personal, compassionate concern. But when strengthened, comforted, and encouraged, we are to remember that God's help is given to us so that we, in turn, may help others. Not ponds but channels, not trophies alone but instruments of grace, we are to follow the example of our Lord, of whom we read, "For in that He Himself has suffered, being tempted, He is able to aid those who are tempted" (Heb. 2:18).

It should be borne in mind that the best help we may give is to aid the troubled, confused, or sorrowing soul to look not to us, but to God. Some people want a human helper to lean upon in times of trouble, and many others are willing to be such a source of help. Put two persons such as these together, and an insidious situation can be created. The development of an unhealthy and unscriptural dependence of one upon the other results in greater weakness rather than strength.

## SPIRITUAL SPLENDOR IN SUFFERING

Spiritual splendor fills verse 5 as it speaks of the sufferings of Christ abounding in Paul. Throughout his epistles we can glimpse the fierceness—even horror—of the apostle's sufferings (notably in that catalog of calamities listed in 2 Corinthians 11: 23–33), which he endured *for* Christ (as in Phil. 1:13: ". . . my chains are in Christ . . ."). Here, however, Paul instills an even more exalted meaning: He was suffering *with* Christ—

"sharing abundantly in Christ's sufferings," as it is sometimes so well translated. The pains of hunger, thirst, and homelessness, suffered by Christ, are ones His servant Paul also claimed for himself (1 Cor. 4:11–13): ". . . we both hunger and thirst, and we are poorly clothed, beaten, and homeless. . . . Being reviled . . . being persecuted . . . being defamed. . . ." He did not suggest that his sufferings were as great, nor that they were redemptive as were those of his Lord, but he did accept them as a means of sharing with Christ the awful burden He bore for our salvation. Paul was thus brought a deep comfort: ". . . so our consolation also abounds by Christ."

We are not now taught to value this consolation which comes with sharing the sufferings of Christ. Much is said about the helpful and happy results of being Christian—which are real and should be discussed—but one is not apt to hear that "to you it has been granted on behalf of Christ, not only to believe in Him, but also to suffer for His sake" (Phil. 1:29). Indeed some feel that suffering for Christ suggests a reduced Christianity, a feeble faith, and a craven spirit. The apostles of whom we read in Acts 5 would not have understood such a debasing of the willingness to suffer. They, having been beaten and commanded by the council not to speak in the name of Jesus, ". . . departed . . . rejoicing that they were counted worthy to suffer shame for His [Jesus'] name" (Acts 5:41). And, risking further beatings or worse indignities, ". . . they did not cease teaching and preaching Jesus as the Christ" (v. 42). That was the spirit of Paul. ". . . The Holy Spirit testifies in every city," he wrote in Acts 20:23,24, "saying that chains and tribulations await me. But none of these things move me; nor do I count my life dear to myself. . . ." His supreme desire was that ". . . Christ . . . be magnified in my body, whether by life or by death" (Phil. 1:20).

The afflictions through which some people pass do not have this effect on them; they are left blighted, spiritually desiccated, and bitter. Wherever they go they spread depression and gloom, lamenting their lot and censuring both God and man for their misfortunes. Not so with Paul. His many adversities were borne in such a way that the churches were inspired and encouraged to believe that, in their own trials, they too would be divinely sustained. Thus the apostle's hardships provided not only the occasion for him personally to test and prove the promises of God, but to demonstrate to his spiritual charges the divine faithfulness.

James cited the prophets, ". . . who have spoken in the name of the Lord, as an example of suffering and patience. Indeed, we count them blessed who endure . . ." (James 5:10,11). Surely the people of God in all generations count the apostle Paul blessed not only for the divine wisdom with which he wrote and the dauntless spirit with which he proclaimed the gospel, but also for the magnificent way in which he endured hardship.

A lovely expression of both gratification and generosity is found in verse 7, where Paul wrote, "And our hope for you is steadfast [unshaken] . . . ." His relations with the Corinthian church had undergone a severe strain while the seditious Judaizers had spread their doctrinal poison. It may not be an exaggeration to say that an outright rebellion on the part of many had been fomented against the apostle. Now, with the unpleasantness past, Paul expressed his confidence that the Corinthians were once again committed to ". . . the gospel which was preached by me, . . ." as he wrote of his message in Galatians 1:11.

We may be sure that Paul was relieved that the tension between the Corinthians and himself had been resolved. A person of sensitivity to whom any disruption of agreeable relations would be painful, he must have been especially upset by the situation in the church at Corinth. He had founded that church, ". . . teaching the Word of God among them" for eighteen months (Acts 18:11), guiding them out of the idolatry and immorality in which they had lived and into the light and loveliness of Christian faith. Their defection from true doctrine and their disavowal of Paul as God's chosen messenger must have grieved him deeply.

At the same time, though, his gratitude that the Corinthians had recovered from the spiritual and doctrinal delinquency threatening the very life of the church was deeper than his grief. However precious he felt the Corinthians' relationship to himself to be, he knew their faith in Christ was supremely important. Paul disclaimed any right to place his needs equal to that faith, as he made clear in 1:24: "Not that we have dominion [lord it] over your faith. . . ."

We may believe, too, that the Corinthians were heartened by Paul's expression of confidence. Feelings of guilt would have been natural for them, and they must have appreciated the generous words, "Our hope for you is unshaken. . . ." Such gentle, tactful opening lines no doubt made the rest of the epistle easier to write for Paul, and more instructive and encouraging to the Corinthians. The so-called "stern letter" must have been—and needed to be—corrective, but these tender words show an invincible goodwill, beautifully suitable for dispelling tension and restoring the loving fellowship between the apostle and the Corinthians.

# 2

## PARTNERS IN PRAYER

*2 Cor. 1:8–11*

**8** For we do not want you to be ignorant, brethren, of our trouble which came to us in Asia: that we were burdened beyond measure, above strength, so that we despaired even of life. **9** But we had the sentence of death in ourselves, that we should not trust in ourselves but in God who raises the dead, **10** who delivered us from so great a death, and does deliver us; in whom we trust that He will still deliver us, **11** you also helping together by prayer for us, that thanks may be given by many persons on our behalf for the gift granted to us through many.

Here we find a glimpse of the distressing experiences which came to Paul in fulfilling his apostolic commission. "We do not want you to be ignorant, brethren," he wrote, "of our trouble which came to us in Asia. . . ." What that "trouble" was, we do not know. Perhaps he referred to the uproar instigated by Demetrius, of which we read in Acts 19. Perhaps instead he referred to an illness, or to his mental and spiritual distress caused by the antagonism of the Corinthian church. Even though *we* do not know, the Corinthians probably *did* know the nature of the ordeal through which Paul had passed. That he wrote in such a way, with so few details, suggests that he saw no point in repeating facts already well known.

Furthermore, the exact nature of the trouble, even if it were unknown to the Corinthians, is not important here; Paul's purpose was to emphasize the *spiritual result* of the trouble, not the *details* of his pain. To do so, however, he had to underline the frightful nature of the experience, that it had been one in which he was "burdened beyond measure, above strength, so that [he] despaired even of life."As he had considered the outcome, while enduring the trouble, death seemed the only solution. Indeed, the expression "sentence of death" is literally "answer of death." He was, as one translation puts it, "utterly, unbearably crushed," brought down so low that the only conceivable way out was death.

This nightmarish torment, whatever or whoever brought it upon Paul, proved to be to his abundant advantage, for it forced him to reassert his need of reliance upon God. ". . . we should not trust in ourselves but in God. . . ." This is a lesson which he had learned before—a certainty upon which his life and labors rested—but it is also a truth he needed to be reminded of in this fearful trial.

This absolute reliance on God is one of those spiritual principles which are known to us intellectually but which can only be truly apprehended and tested in difficult, threatening circumstances in which we no longer can claim control over our lives.

Grace for living, traveling, teaching, and serving had been given daily to Paul. He recognized, and rejoiced in, the capacity to be abased or to abound, to ". . . do all things through Christ who strengthens me," as he told the Philippians (4:13). Still, the ultimate application of his reliance on God could only come in a place of such darkness, a situation of such dreadfulness, that he must have extraordinary help, must realize his own inadequacy, and must rely on the "God who raises the dead." Great stress is the final—and the most trustworthy—test of the strength of a man's beliefs, and in that crucible Paul's faith proved strong.

## NOT COMFORTABLE, BUT CONFORMABLE

Any trial, however severe, which brings us to the place where we cast ourselves upon the grace and mercy of God is a blessing. Grievous though it may be, ". . . nevertheless, afterward it yields the peaceable [or peaceful] fruit of righteousness to those who have been trained by it" (Heb. 12:11). God has given us life, and particularly life in Christ, so that we may achieve and create goodness, not so that we can enjoy ourselves. We belittle our faith when we make of it a means to escape the rigors of life. We tarnish it by failing to see that the divine plan is not to make us *comfortable*, but *conformable* to God's will and ". . . partakers of His holiness" (Heb. 12:10).

The ordeal benefited Paul, not only because it drove him to trust in God but also because it afforded him the privilege of seeing the power of God deliver him. One old and cherished saying could well express the feelings of the apostle as he looked back on this experience: "Man's extremity is God's opportunity." His soul was soaring with joy that, in this fearful predicament, God needed only to hear his cry and see his faith and He would deliver him.

## DELIVERANCE

Moreover, Paul could face the present and future in stronger faith, having been delivered "from so great a death." He had learned that God ". . . does deliver us . . . [and] will still deliver us." What he had experienced of God's love and care in the past gave him assurance that the same divine concern could be depended upon in the present—and in the future. With no giddy, heady words, though, did Paul express this confidence. He did not consider himself such a superior figure in the church that he had no need for the prayers of his fellow Christians. Instead, he proclaimed that very need.

Paul's request for their "helping together by prayer for us" could have been another generous, but oblique, expression of his confidence in them, his assurance that their estrangement from him was over. His thankfulness at his deliverance was increased by their sharing of that joy and by their renewed prayer for him.

Similarly, no Christian relationship is healthy unless it is a partnership of prayer, one for the other. It follows that any disruption of that fellowship can be remedied most effectively by the simple means of praying together. Thus, Paul's call to the Corinthians to pray for him, with his implied confidence in their willingness to do so and in the effectiveness of their prayers, must have been a helpful factor in solving the distressing problems in the Corinthian church.

# 3

# PAUL'S INTEGRITY

*2 Cor. 1:12–2:2*
    **12** For our boasting is this: the testimony of our con-
science that we conducted ourselves in the world in simplicity and godly sincerity, not with fleshly wisdom but by the
grace of God, and more abundantly toward you. **13** For we
are not writing any other things to you than what you read or
understand; and I trust you will understand even to the end
**14** (as also you have understood us in part), that we are your
boast as you also are ours, in the day of the Lord Jesus.

The word "boast," in the sense in which it is used today, is not a
word we are comfortable attributing to the apostle Paul. He
wrote with such artless modesty of himself in so many places
that we cannot conceive of him indulging in vain swaggering.
Perhaps this is why the scholars who produced the original King
James Version could not bring themselves to use the translation
"boasting" in verse 12. They chose instead to make it read "For
our *rejoicing* is this. . . ." The Revised Version, perhaps for the
same reason, used "glorying" rather than "boasting."
    Still, the most legitimate translation of the Greek is "boast-
ing," even though here the word carries no implications of
pride or conceit. Paul was simply expressing the fact that,
contrary to the accusations of his opponents, he had lived a life
of holiness and godly sincerity before all men and, especially,
before the Corinthians. His glorying in such a life was something he was *entitled* to do, and it must have been extremely
gratifying to him.

## A CLEAR CONSCIENCE

The person who knows himself and knows that his motives

are worthy, his integrity above question, his acts and words honorable and sincere, is one who possesses a precious security. I once received a letter which was unpleasant to read; but I received great satisfaction in being able to answer that letter with these words: "Whatever your feelings may be about my integrity, I have absolutely no doubt about it." I believe this is similar to the way Paul felt as he wrote, "For our boasting is this: the testimony of our conscience. . . ."

In his conduct while with the Corinthians and in what he said to them in his letters, his conscience testified that he had acted and written, not in earthly, human wisdom but in holiness, godly sincerity, and by the grace of God. Many readers take the position that he was *defending* himself and his integrity, but it seems more likely that he was expressing a positive confidence in himself. Paul would probably agree with an opinion of this writer, that those who must constantly affirm their sincerity, who "protest too much," are the very ones whose honesty should be questioned. To be accused of deviousness was unpleasant, even painful, but Paul's rebuttal was simply "the testimony of his conscience." His actions stood by themselves and needed no words of his to camouflage or explain them.

15 And in this confidence I intended to come to you before, that you might have a second benefit—16 to pass by way of you to Macedonia, to come again from Macedonia to you, and be helped by you on my way to Judea. 17 Therefore, when I was planning this, did I do it lightly? Or the things I plan, do I plan according to the flesh, that with me there should be Yes, Yes and No, No? 18 But as God is faithful, our word to you was not Yes and No. 19 For the Son of God, Jesus Christ, who was preached among you by us—by me, Silvanus, and Timothy—was not Yes and No, but in Him was Yes. 20 For all the promises of God in Him are Yes, and in Him Amen, to the glory of God by us. 21 Now He who establishes us with you in Christ and has anointed us is God, 22 who also has sealed us and given us the Spirit in our hearts as a deposit. 23 Moreover I call God as witness against my

soul, that to spare you I came no more to Corinth. **24** Not that we have dominion over your faith, but are fellow workers for your joy; for by faith you stand.

**1** But I determined this within myself, that I would not come again to you in sorrow. **2** For if I make you sorrowful, then who is he who makes me glad but the one who is made sorrowful by me?

It is perhaps unfortunate that the term "epistles" is used to describe Paul's writings, rather than "letters." We think of epistles as theological discourses—which Paul's writings were, in a sense—but their essential purpose was more as *letters*, written to deal with specific situations, to answer particular questions, and to correct evident errors.

## SPARING THE CHURCH

In this part of his letter the apostle dealt with some adverse comments made concerning his change of plans about coming to Corinth in person. He "intended to come," he said, both on the way to Macedonia and on his return from there. He was confident that he could do this, he wrote, but it simply did not work out as he had planned. Why make so much of it? No one can guarantee that his plans are not subject to change for one reason or another.

The apostle showed splendid restraint as he dealt with the petty criticisms of his altered itinerary. His plans were not made "according to the flesh," he stated, to be followed on a basis of "yes and no"—"yes" at one moment and then, in a frivolous manner, "no" the next. Instead, his life was under the dominion of the Son of God, in whom all the promises of God were "yes" and "amen." It was to spare them that he changed his plans: "I determined . . . that I would not come again to you in sorrow." Evidently Paul had visited Corinth previously, seeking to correct their faltering, and, we may suspect, to face his Judaizing opponents in person. That visit had not been success-

ful; it was painful for all concerned, and the apostle had no wish
to repeat such an experience.

## IN CHRIST

In the midst of these explanations appear several verses
glowing with spiritual meaning. Verse 20 declares that "all the
promises of God in Him [Christ] are Yes, and in [through]
Him Amen to the glory of God by us." It is glorious to know
that, as we seek assurance that God's promises to us may be
fulfilled in our lives, in Christ we see the answer—Yes! And it is
immeasurably reassuring to know that, through Christ, we may
answer Amen to His promises. We believe them and receive
them, as we answer the question, "Will God act, love, help,
save, sustain . . . ?" with a joyous Amen. It is as though God,
in Christ, says "Yes," and we, through Christ, respond
"Amen!"

Verses 21 and 22 delineate four beautiful spiritual truths: In
Christ the believer is "established" in the midst of fickleness
and instability, ". . . able to stand against the wiles of the
devil" (Eph. 6:11). In Christ the believer is also "anointed,"
divinely set apart, commissioned, and enabled to live and to
serve to the glory of God. Furthermore, in Christ the believer is
"sealed," given the stamp of God's possession, made uniquely
and eternally His own. And, finally, in Christ the believer is
given the Holy Spirit as a "deposit," a guarantee that the
Christian can count on God's presence now and will one day
enter into His full, eternal inheritance.

# 4

# THE BEAUTY OF FORGIVENESS

*2 Cor. 2:3–11*

**3** And I wrote this very thing to you, lest, when I came, I should have sorrow over those from whom I ought to have joy, having confidence in you all that my joy is the joy of you all. **4** For out of much affliction and anguish of heart I wrote to you, with many tears, not that you should be grieved, but that you might know the love which I have so abundantly for you. **5** But if anyone has caused grief, he has not grieved me, but to some extent—not to be too severe—all of you. **6** This punishment which was inflicted by the majority is sufficient for such a man, **7** so that, on the contrary, you ought rather to forgive and comfort him, lest perhaps such a one be swallowed up with too much sorrow. **8** Therefore I urge you to confirm your love to him. **9** For to this end I also wrote, that I might put you to the test, whether you are obedient in all things. **10** Now whom you forgive anything, I also forgive. For if indeed I have forgiven anything, whom I have forgiven I have forgiven it for your sakes in the presence of Christ, **11** lest Satan should take advantage of us; for we are not ignorant of his devices.

Among the great words in which our Christian gospel is expressed, *forgiveness* takes its place at or near the summit in terms of importance and beauty. The very heart of the gospel is the blessed fact that God, in Christ, has forgiven all who will trust in Jesus as Savior and acknowledge Him as Lord of their lives. There is a second part to this lesson of forgiveness, however, since the gospel also lays upon the heart and conscience of anyone divinely forgiven the duty and privilege of forgiving others, "even as God for Christ's sake has forgiven [him]."

## FREELY FORGIVE

The above quoted verses apply the gospel's instruction concerning forgiveness to the specific situation of someone guilty of a grievous offense against the apostle Paul, and, as well, against the entire Corinthian church. Paul, consistent with his innate courtesy and consideration, minimized the measure in which he had been wronged. Having freely forgiven the guilty man, he is concerned lest the church fail to do so.

Who was the offender? Some scholars suggest the man guilty of incest for whom Paul prescribed stern discipline in chapter 5 of his first epistle. Others believe it was someone who had instigated a rebellion against the apostle and had thus committed not only an offense against him but against the church. Paul did not say who it was or what he had done. His attitude was one of affectionate concern for the welfare of the church and for the now punished, repentant, and sorrowing offender.

Punishment had been inflicted "by the majority" (v. 6). Some Corinthians—for reasons we do not know but can imagine—apparently did not feel the chastisement was sufficient. But the punishment had been "sufficient," wrote Paul, and it was time to forgive, lest the offender be overcome, "swallowed up with too much sorrow."

There may be no greater loneliness than to be rejected by one's own. The pitiful lament of Cain, sentenced to be a fugitive and wanderer for the murder of his brother, comes down to us through the centuries to haunt us with its pathetic despair: "My punishment is greater than I can bear!" This man of Corinth, too, must have felt abandoned, accursed, as he was denied the fellowship of the saints and barred from the warmth and love he had once known.

## REAFFIRMING LOVE, RESTORING FELLOWSHIP

Sometimes withholding discipline from one guilty of sin simply aids and abets him in his wrongdoing. Other times, if forgiveness is withheld or given partially or grudgingly, the offender either becomes hardened, driven into incorrigibility, or is overcome with guilt and remorse so great that he surrenders to despair and hopelessness. Paul saw this penitent offender on the brink of such anguish and called on the church to "forgive" him, to "comfort" him, and to "confirm [their] love" to him.

One of the decisive tests of our Christianity is the manner in which we follow our Lord's command to forgive. If our chief concern is appeasement, at the cost of the humbling—even humiliation—of the offender, we have not even approached the forgiveness the Lord requires of us. Christian forgiveness is far more than accepting an apology—more, even, than putting away vengeful feelings. To truly forgive means not to require, nor to find satisfaction in, seeing someone grovel in remorse and contrition. One's principal concern should not be one's own rights, but rather finding a means of ending the estrangement and restoring fellowship.

It is said that Moravian missionaries to the Eskimos found no word for forgiveness in the native language, so they "manufactured" one—*Issumagijonjungnainermik.* Formidable looking, perhaps, but the word carries a beautiful meaning: "Not-being-able-to-think-about-it-anymore." This literal translation may answer the question some ask, "We can forgive, but can we truly forget?" We may not be able—most of us are not able—to put the *facts* out of our memory, but the Spirit of Christ enables us not to think about them any more, surely not to think vindictively about them.

## SATAN'S "DEVICES"

When a part of the physical body is injured, all of the rest of the body is involved in healing the wound. The use of the resources of other parts of the body to end the pain of one member is analogous to what happens in the church, since the church is described by Paul as being the body of Christ with its members, ". . . members of one another" (Rom. 12:5). Thus, when one member is injured, it is the privilege and mission of others to restore him.

Paul was aware that, lurking nearby, Satan was seeking to plunge this particular offender into despair, hoping to displace his honest repentance with hopeless remorse, so that he would be driven away from the family of faith entirely. This would have been tragic, for that individual and for all the church. Since we are members of one another, if one suffers all suffer; the banishment of one is a dismemberment of a body made sacred by the sacrifice of Christ. This fact, crucial though it is, does not receive adequate recognition. As a result, Satan's "devices" are sometimes eminently successful. He takes advantage of a churlish, unforgiving attitude wherever he finds it to dishearten the penitent and drive him away.

Once a young, unstable Christian, returning in sorrow to ask forgiveness of a church group for a foolish (but not disgraceful) lapse in conduct, was severely rebuked by the leader of the group. Brokenhearted, he fled to wander in a spiritual wilderness for years. In that one heartless act of driving a penitent away, that leader's preaching of many years was discredited and abased. The advantage was Satan's, the greatest loss was mine, for I was that young Christian humiliated in the name of holiness who thus lost the blessing of many years of Christian living.

# 5

# TRIUMPHANT IN CHRIST

*2 Cor. 2:12–17*
   **12** Furthermore, when I came to Troas to preach Christ's gospel, and a door was opened to me by the Lord, **13** I had no rest in my spirit, because I did not find Titus my brother; but taking my leave of them, I went from there to Macedonia. **14** Now thanks be to God who always leads us in triumph in Christ, and makes manifest the aroma of His knowledge by us in every place. **15** For we are to God the fragrance of Christ among those who are being saved and among those who are perishing. **16** To the one we are the aroma of death to death, and to the other the aroma of life to life. And who is sufficient for these things? **17** For we are not, as so many, peddling the word of God; but as of sincerity, but as from God, we speak in the sight of God in Christ.

Someone has perceptively noted that what we need for living effectively is to know not merely what to *do,* but what to do *next.* All of us get caught in quandaries where we are forced to choose, not between a good and a bad course of action, but between good and best. The apostle Paul was faced with such a problem. He had gone to Troas ". . . to preach Christ's gospel, and a door was opened to [him ] by the Lord." Certainly this was a propitious situation. He had come to preach and God had given him the opportunity to reach people's hearts. So great was his concern for the Corinthians, though, so troubled was his mind by Titus' failing to bring him hoped-for tidings, that he left Troas and went to Macedonia.

## LOVING CONCERN

   Some commentators have passed harsh judgment upon Paul for turning from this opportunity in Troas, calling his anxiety

and restlessness weakness. I disagree, as do others such as F. W.
Farrar, who seems indignant, if not outraged, at the "spirit of
superfluous disquisition and idle letter-worship" with which
some have "ventured to discuss whether St. Paul was justified in
neglecting this opportunity. . . . To say that he ought to have
had strength of mind enough to get the mastery over his feelings
is only to say that Paul ought not to have been Paul."* The
apostle was no mechanical man, serving his Lord as a robot. He
is in fact endeared to us precisely for his capacity for deep
human feelings. It is to his *credit* that he was so lovingly
concerned about the Corinthian situation that he could not
"rest in his spirit" until he knew that the problems there had
been resolved.

As these lines are written, my brother is recuperating from
surgery for a large, cancerous tumor in his brain. All of the
cancer could not be excised, and, apart from divine help, there
is no hope. Most people understand how difficult it is for me to
carry on my ministry and do my work as though I had no
concern for Robert. The church at Corinth was *spiritually*
rather than physically crippled, so it was even harder for Paul to
concentrate on other things as he would normally do, because
of his distress over them. Moreover, Paul's work at Troas was
not unproductive, nor was his time there wasted. Returning
later, he found a vigorous church—evidence that the seed sown
in weakness had brought forth a harvest, to the glory of God
and, in at least some measure, the vindication of His servant
Paul.

## CONQUERED AND CAPTIVE

Verse 14 seems built on an abrupt change in tone from verses
12 and 13. Actually, Paul burst into a doxology here for the
triumph which followed his distress. What seemed to be defeat

---

*The Pulpit Commentary: II Corinthians (Grand Rapids, Mich.: Eerdmans, 1959), p. 39.

was shown to be victory, and he was full of praise. He employed a figure, to express that praise, which would have been well understood by those to whom he wrote. A triumphal march by a conqueror, a procession of victors and victims, was a common sight in those days. The march symbolized the privilege of sharing the conqueror's glory, which belonged to the victors, and the death or captivity awaiting the vanquished. Laden with the perfume of incense, the air would have been filled with shouts of victory and praise.

Paul saw himself—and all believers—as having been conquered by God and as privileged to be His captives. Often in his writings Paul referred to himself as "the prisoner of Christ," speaking of his bondage to his Lord with joy. God had conquered him—as He has conquered us—not by force but by love. The weapon used was the cross, upon which He gave His beloved Son to die for our sins. And now we, once His enemies and now His trophies, march in His train, the "triumphant captives" of the Lord!

Verses 15 and 16 extend the metaphor of the triumphal parade. The fragrance of incense in the procession would have been pleasant to the victors but sinister to those conquered, for it was a token of death to them. So the gospel preached by Paul—and by all who proclaim it by the enabling grace of God—is to believers ". . . the power of God to salvation . . ." (Rom. 1:16); but to those who reject it, it becomes the sentence of death.

The question, "And who is sufficient for these things?" is not the abrupt and rhetorical insertion it may seem to be. Paul is thinking of the great and eternal consequences of preaching and hearing the gospel. Who could be adequate, in himself, to carry this "message angels fain would sing"? Not he, not of himself, of that he was sure. He identified himself as "the chief of sinners," "the least of the apostles," who only by the grace of God was called to preach "the unsearchable riches of Christ." Verse 3:5 contains the only answer to the question Paul would

have found possible: "Not that we are sufficient of ourselves
. . . but our sufficiency is from God."

Verse 17 deals with a problem church people have faced ever
since the day of Paul: the accusations of cynics that honorable
servants of Christ were making merchandise of the gospel. A
number of Greek scholars tell us that the word translated
"corrupt" in the King James Version, and "peddling" in the
New King James Bible, is more accurately translated
"hucksterizing." This choice of terms makes verse 17 even
more offensive, suggesting that Paul was accused of making the
Word of God a huckster's goods, adulterated and contaminated
by his dishonesty and greed. Paul refused to be tarred with such
a stick. He spoke here, as he already had in 1:12, of the
testimony of his own conscience that he was sincere, speaking
". . . in the sight of God in Christ." No one felt greater
contempt than he for those who made merchandise of sacred
truth, whose touch of consecrated things was a sacrilegious
defilement. Such an accusation could not withstand a moment's honest scrutiny nor rise against Paul before God.

# 6

## THE AUTOGRAPH OF GOD

*2 Cor. 3:1–6*

**1** Do we begin again to commend ourselves? Or do we need, as some others, epistles of commendation to you or letters of commendation from you? **2** You are our epistle written in our hearts, known and read by all men, **3** inasmuch as you are manifestly declared to be an epistle of Christ, ministered by us, written not with ink but by the Spirit of the living God, not on tablets of stone but on tablets of flesh, that is, of the heart. **4** And we have such trust through Christ toward God. **5** Not that we are sufficient of ourselves to think of anything as being from ourselves, but our sufficiency is from God, **6** who also has made us sufficient as ministers of the new covenant, not of the letter but of the Spirit; for the letter kills, but the Spirit gives life.

It was a custom, and perhaps a necessity, for Christians in Paul's time to carry letters of identification and recommendation when they traveled. With Christianity considered "a new and illegal religion," under suspicion and surveillance, groups of believers had to protect themselves by seeing that newcomers were recommended by the church from which they had come. Carrying credentials would be especially important, of course, for those who came to teach. When Apollos, for example, determined to leave Ephesus and go to Achaia (probably Corinth), "the brethren wrote, exhorting the disciples [to which he was going] to receive him."

### LIVING LETTERS

Paul, however, felt he did not need to carry such credentials to the Corinthians: "Do I, whom you know so well, and know of my love for you, and faithful ministry to you, need a letter of recommendation to you, or from you? *You* are our letter of recommendation for everyone to read." Obviously the Judaistic teachers who had caused such mischief in the Corinthian church had brought such letters (written, it is also evident, by those who should have been more selective in their sanctions). The use these men made of the letters—to destroy and defame—proved that such pieces of paper could not always be trusted to recommend good men.

Those who proclaim the gospel are expected to be educated in general matters, as well as in theology. A good appearance, attractive personality, pleasing voice, and other qualities are also advantageous. Above all, though, those who minister must have unassailable character and the confidence of those to whom they are sent. Paul knew his own character, but he was concerned about the personal attacks which could undermine the confidence of the Corinthians and thus inhibit his proclamation of God's message. Rather than looking in epistles for proofs of his sincerity and the force of his message, Paul asked the Corinthians to look at his actions and also at themselves. The apostle was thus reminding them of a supremely important truth which should be borne in mind by Christians of all ages. Each Corinthian, by his lifestyle, either affirmed the credibility of the gospel or denied its effect. The same is true today. While some people will refuse to acknowledge the power of the gospel, whatever testimony is offered to them, many will accept transformed lives as the autograph of God. At the same time, carnality in the life of a professing Christian is perceived as indicative of the questionable worth of the gospel. Whether we like it or not, we are epistles ". . . known and read by all men."

## SOMETHING BETTER

At the initiation of the old covenant, God wrote on tablets of stone venerable commandments which were to shape moral thought and guide legal, ethical, and religious processes for the following centuries. Christ Jesus, wrote Paul, now provides a better priest, ". . . a more excellent ministry . . . a better covenant, which was established on better promises" (Heb. 8:6)—written, not on stone, but on hearts.

The Law was a table of commands, regulations, and ordinances based on the permissibility of actions. Leviticus 18:5 expressed the basis of the Law: "Ye shall therefore keep my statutes, and my judgments, which, if a man do, he shall live in them. . . ." Paul documented the strength of the old Law and drew a sharp contrast between it and the new covenant by quoting from Leviticus 18:5 in several places, such as in Romans 10:5: "Moses writes about the righteousness which is of the law, 'The man who does those things shall live by [through] them' " and in Galatians 3:12. The contrast lies in the fact that the new covenant, written in the heart, reaches far beyond actions. David Thomas, in *The Pulpit Commentary*, writes luminously about Christianity written on the heart, saying that it is the most *legible* form, the most *convincing* form, the most *persuasive* form, the most *enduring* form, and the *divinest* form of Christianity.* Indeed, unless written in our hearts, the validity of our Christian commitment is always in doubt.

I see verse 4 as a kind of commitment. The apostle Paul put the matter of his acceptance by the Corinthians into the hands of God. He saw no benefit in brooding over the matter, knowing that, of himself, his strength was not sufficient either to bring anyone to or establish anyone in faith. God was, and is, sufficient, though (vv. 5,6), and made Paul a minister of the new covenant.

Paul made clear that what had taken place in the hearts of the Corinthian Christians came about through the grace and power of God. "Our sufficiency is of God," he wrote. His

---

*The Pulpit Commentary: II Corinthians* (Grand Rapids, Mich.: Eerdmans, 1959), p. 62.

ministry, as he indicated elsewhere, notably in chapter 12, was
more than he could accomplish by himself. He was dependent
upon divine grace, that enabling energy of God which makes
the weak able to "do all things through Christ." Paul knew his
strength would grow only in so far as he recognized his own
weakness and reliance on God.

However, Paul did *not* say he was insufficient, period. He was
"*made* sufficient" by the indwelling power of the Spirit of God,
ministering ". . . not of the letter but of the [Holy] Spirit.
. . ." He concerned himself, not with technicalities, rules,
verbal and legal proprieties, but with the life-giving, life-
enriching, power-bestowing Spirit. We take a crucial, blessed,
liberating step in Christian life and service when we comprehend this vital truth.

# 7

## FROM GLORY TO GLORY

*2 Cor. 3:7–18*
**7** But if the ministry of death, written and engraved on stones, was glorious, so that the children of Israel could not look steadily at the face of Moses because of the glory of his countenance, which glory was passing away, **8** how will the ministry of the Spirit not be more glorious? **9** For if the ministry of condemnation had glory, the ministry of righteousness exceeds much more in glory. **10** For even what was made glorious had no glory in this respect, because of the glory that excels. **11** For if what is passing away was glorious, what remains is much more glorious. **12** Seeing then that we have such hope, we use great boldness of speech— **13** unlike Moses, who put a veil over his face so that the children of Israel could not look steadily at the end of what was passing away. **14** But their minds were hardened. For until this day the same veil remains unlifted in the reading of the Old Testament, because the veil is taken away in Christ. **15** But even to this day, when Moses is read, a veil lies on their heart. **16** Nevertheless when one turns to the Lord, the veil is taken away. **17** Now the Lord is the Spirit; and where the Spirit of the Lord is, there is liberty. **18** But we all, with unveiled face, beholding as in a mirror the glory of the Lord, are being transformed into the same image from glory to glory, just as by the Spirit of the Lord.

Writers have drawn attention to the fact that the apostle Paul, in his writings, frequently leaped from one thought to another, changed metaphors abruptly, and seemed little concerned with syntax. This passage might appear to uphold this criticism. Why did Paul shift from comments of a personal nature to what seems to be an extraneous dissertation concerning the contrast between "the letter" (Law) and "Spirit" (the Lord)? Clearly Paul, having mentioned the new covenant of which he was a minister, felt impelled to elaborate on the glorious nature of that covenant, to stress its superiority and advantages over the old covenant of works.

## THE NONNEGOTIABLE COVENANT

A covenant, especially between God and man, differs from a contract or agreement between two people, in which each party is entitled to determine the conditions. When God offers to man a covenant, the terms are nonnegotiable, to be accepted or rejected as they are. When Moses, his face aglow, came down from his meeting with God, he presented the covenant of the Law to Israel. The people, in what some scholars think was a spirit of rash self-confidence, responded, "All that the Lord hath said will we do, and be obedient" (Ex. 24:7). The Law was not imposed upon them until they willingly accepted it, but after that its terms were irrevocably binding.

Note what Paul said of that covenant. He called it a "ministry [some prefer 'dispensation'] of death" and "of condemnation," and we can see the justice of those descriptions. At its inception, Moses' face was aglow; yet the Law, once broken, prescribed death in numerous cases. The tabernacle and temple, once described as "vast slaughterhouses," were steeped in blood from sacrifices offered in place of offenders against God. Such strictness and insistence on retribution manifested God's abhorrence of sin and are examples of the measures He took to teach us the intensity of His holy hatred of it.

Paul insisted, however, that even though the Law was a ministry of death and condemnation, it was at the same time a "glorious" covenant. We have seen how Moses brought it back to Israel with a countenance so translucent with the glory of God that people could not look at him. Whatever the fearsome penalties for the Law's violation, it was still a magnificent arrangement between God and His people—an arrangement which governed the conduct and guided the morals of this remarkable society. God's use of its strictures to reveal to men their moral and spiritual inability to please Him, thus leading them to Christ (see Gal. 3:24), makes those commands even more glorious. Such a law could not be brushed aside as trash; it was replaced when Christ came, because by His taking on the likeness of sinful flesh, the new covenant did what the Law was unable to do: fulfill "the *righteous* requirement of the law . . . in us . . ." (Rom. 8:4).

## THE NEW COVENANT

Paul described the new covenant simply as "*more* glorious," "much more in glory," "the glory that excels," etc. This covenant is "not written and engraved on stones" but is on the heart. It is a covenant of life; when we embrace it, we pass from death to life and become not only partakers of divine life but also of the divine nature. A veil covers the hearts of those who persist in living under the old covenant which is only taken away when one turns to the Lord. What a terrible tragedy that so many eyes and hearts remain veiled, blind to the riches which God has offered us in Christ. We can imagine the deep feelings with which Paul wrote these words as we recall what he said to the Romans: ". . . I have great heaviness and continual sorrow in my heart. For I could wish that I myself were *accursed from Christ* [! ] for my brethren, my kinsmen according to the flesh, who are Israelites . . . of whom are the fathers and from whom, according to the flesh, Christ came. . . ." (Rom. 9:2–5, italics mine).

Verses 17 and 18 are familiar ones, reminding us that ". . . where the Spirit of the Lord is, there is liberty"—freedom from the dominion of death and condemnation, freedom to behold the glory of the Lord and be transformed (gradually and, oh, so slowly!) into the same image, from glory to glory. We are called and enabled by God to leave behind the lesser glories and rise to the supreme splendor, where, at last, "we shall be like Him (1 John 3:2)"!

A crucial phrase here, "with unveiled face," deserves another word. The *privilege* of beholding the glory of the Lord has been bestowed upon every believer, but the *practice* of so doing is incumbent upon us. We forfeit the growth of our souls as we allow our hearts and minds to be veiled by unbelief, by ill will toward others, by carnal habits, by letting our affections become set on lesser things. Whatever else we may want, our supreme desire should be that Christ may be formed in us, that His likeness may be seen in us, His love manifested in us, His will done by us.

# 8

## LIGHT FOR PAUL AND US

*2 Cor. 4:1–6*

1 Therefore, seeing we have this ministry, as we have received mercy, we do not lose heart. 2 But we have renounced the hidden things of shame, not walking in craftiness nor handling the word of God deceitfully, but by manifestation of the truth commending ourselves to every man's conscience in the sight of God. 3 But even if our gospel is veiled, it is veiled to those who are perishing, 4 in whom the god of this age has blinded the minds of those who do not believe, lest the light of the gospel of the glory of Christ, who is the image of God, should shine on them. 5 For we do not preach ourselves, but Christ Jesus the Lord, and ourselves your servants for Jesus' sake. 6 For it is the God who commanded light to shine out of darkness who has shone in our hearts to give the light of the knowledge of the glory of God in the face of Jesus Christ.

It is inspiring to see the strength and stability of a true man of God in difficult situations. Paul, hurt and humiliated as he had been by false and scurrilous charges against him, testified that he still did not lose heart. His utter conviction of the divine bestowment of "this ministry" (of the new covenant) and of its superiority and ultimate triumph allowed him to overcome the opposition of powerful enemies, being forsaken by unstable friends, and being saddened by those indifferent to the good news of God's grace. He had no doubt of his apostolic calling and qualifications, or of his personal fidelity. This certainty, coupled with his recognition of the grace and mercy of God by which he had been chosen as an apostle, gave him courage and assurance, however bleak the outlook might have seemed to others.

## STEADFASTNESS IN TRIAL

To lose heart is a common, very human failing—a perennial temptation to those engaged in spiritual ventures. What Christian worker has been spared the anguish of saying, with the disciples of Jesus, "We have toiled all the night and taken nothing"? Seeing the world plunging at breakneck speed toward catastrophe while facing the frustration of a church seemingly moving as slowly as a glacier—how that tries the soul! Paul must have been tempted—his letters surely indicate the temptation—to give in to frustration, but he met it instead with the affirmation that his labor for the Lord was not in vain.

The divine assignment and enablement were crucial for Paul's steadfastness in trial, but another decisive element was the apostle's own character. There was no room for anything in his life which needed concealment: He had "renounced the hidden things of shame," living, as he had told Governor Felix, with "a conscience without offense toward God and men" (Acts 24:16). The effects of a good conscience can often be seen in peaceful sleep and effective work; the person who, like Paul, instills his actions with unassailable integrity and unwavering faithfulness can stand fearlessly before earth and heaven.

The apostle could also state that he did not "walk in craftiness" nor was he guilty of "handling the Word of God"— that greatest of sacred treasures—"deceitfully." He did not adulterate the gospel to accommodate guilty consciences, nor did he modulate its teaching to support personal views or to avoid controversy. If the church has any constant, authoritative, indispensable guide for its beliefs, hopes, and practices, it is the Word of God. To handle that Word deceptively, to undermine its authority and mute its message, is heresy in the most reprobate form.

## THE NEED FOR SPIRITUAL DISCERNMENT

Paul made clear, in verses 3 and 4, that the gospel is veiled to those who resist it, or find it incomprehensible because they are spiritually blinded and willfully destitute of the power to perceive its truth. When Satan is recognized as god in the place of the true Deity, the mind becomes darkened, incapable of receiving divine truth. Even the gift of intellectual ability does not assure the willingness to accept the spirit of God because the impact of the spirit is spiritually, not mentally, discerned (see 1 Cor. 2:14).

A very important statement appears in verse 5. Paul declared that he preached "Christ Jesus the Lord" ("*as* Lord" is more clearly his meaning) and, secondarily, himself and those who labored with him as "your servants for Jesus' sake." In other words, "Christ is Lord and we are servants, His servants first, and because His, yours." The church of our time needs to become much more aware of this order. The lordship of Christ should be stressed and acknowledged, not merely as a doctrine of Scripture but as a way of living. The roles of minister and servant are congruent, a fact often not recognized now but one our Lord Himself knew well. Ministers, having obtained doctorates and achieved professional recognition, may easily forget that though they are not to be *servile,* they are—primarily—*servants* of Christ and His church. (Actually, the word here translated "servants" is literally "slaves.")

The analogy Paul used in verse 6, based on the account in Genesis of the creation of the heavens and the earth, draws an inspiring truth about man's destiny. The earth is described there as desolate and empty, with a darkness dwelling upon the face of the roaring deep. God, looking upon this desolation and darkness, said, "Let there be light." At His command, the darkness was dispelled and light, without which there could be no life, was shed abroad on the planet. The same God who commanded the light to shine on the earth "has shone in our hearts," wrote Paul, "to give the light of the knowledge of the glory of God in the face of Jesus Christ" to us. Go back and think once again about God's shining in our hearts. In this regard R.V.G. Tasker calls to our attention Chrysostom's poignant remark: "Then indeed He said, Let it be and it was: but now He said nothing, but *Himself* became light for us. . . ."* Do most Christians live in such a manner that anyone would suspect their hearts are filled with such light as this suggests? Or have we allowed our lives to appear "desolate and empty," lacking the luster which should be shining in and through us?

---

*The Second Epistle of Paul to the Corinthians* (Grand Rapids, Mich.: Eerdmans, 1958), p. 72.

# 9

# CAST DOWN BUT UNCONQUERED

2 Cor. 4:7–10
> 7 But we have this treasure in earthen vessels, that the excellence of the power may be of God and not of us. 8 We are hard pressed on every side, yet not crushed; we are perplexed, but not in despair; 9 persecuted, but not forsaken; struck down, but not destroyed— 10 always carrying about in the body the dying of the Lord Jesus, that the life of Jesus may also be manifested in our body.

That God has placed the great treasure of His glory and His gospel in weak human flesh should inspire and uplift us. We ourselves follow a different policy when presenting a gift, especially a costly one: We prefer to enclose such offerings in a handsome case or box (with, if possible, a prestigious maker's or seller's label) with beautiful wrapping. God presents the most magnificent gift of all to us first in the person of a baby in a manger, in a stranger who was despised, rejected, and crucified. He then bestowed the privilege of proclaiming His grace, not upon celestial, magnificent messengers, but upon those who were the recipients of that grace—mere mortals.

Paul often seemed amazed at this choice, certainly as it applied to him. He said he was "the least of the apostles . . . not worthy to be called an apostle" (1 Cor. 15:9), that he was "less than the least of all the saints" (Eph. 3:8). Yet, because his call was a gift of grace, he never questioned his right to be *acknowledged* as an apostle. He was certain of his commission to be a minister of the new covenant, but was also constantly aware that this treasure was carried about, by him and all who received it, in "earthen vessels." It is incredible to our human minds that God would use mere mortals as His evangels. Even a partial understanding of our limitations, which is all we have, makes us realize our unworthiness to touch this treasure.

## BEWARE OF THE "CELEBRITY SYNDROME"

A proper recognition and honor should be given to those who have served our Lord and mankind with extraordinary effectiveness. Let us never forget, however, that the greatest of us is only a vessel, and "the excellence of the power [is ] of God. . . ." The "celebrity syndrome," which exalts people simply because they are well known in professional fields of activity, is a trap which impedes their development. Many such famous people, newly converted, have found fledgling faith and "green grace" too shaky to withstand the pressure of those who, whether simply to introduce them as Christians or to exploit them, have cast them into deep waters. Paul's command in 1 Timothy 5:22, "Do not lay hands on anyone hastily . . . ," is seen by some as an order not to ordain persons for special service until they have proven themselves. Others consider it an injunction against the restoration of those who are not yet restored in their hearts. In either case, Paul forbade precipitous action. The apostle himself, scholarly theologian that he was, spent three years in Arabia in preparation for the ministry he was to perform.

## A COLLISION COURSE WITH THE WORLD

Good people who feel that the Christian life is intended to provide immunity from the harsh realities of living should study these four verses carefully. If we feel that our faith is given us simply to put us beyond the reach of any possible incubus, sooner or later hard realities will compel us to abandon that fiction. Christian living is *not* a sheltered exemption, *not* an easy immunity from the assaults of life. God does *not* promise that. He *does* promise, and provide, His own enabling strength and overcoming grace, whatever our lot may be. He assures us of His abiding peace, but not a peace which must depend upon peaceful conditions around us. His promise is made with the noise of conflict and the hammering of tribulation as an accompaniment. The glory is in the calm at the center in spite of the sometimes terrifying turbulence at the circumference.

The apostle, when commenting on his own experience, testified to this truth: "We are hard pressed . . . perplexed . . . persecuted . . . struck down," he says, ". . . yet not crushed . . . not in despair . . . not forsaken . . . not destroyed." The nuances of meaning involved in this affirmation are unimportant. The essential fact Paul communicated was that the *stress* he had to face was never greater than the *strength* he was given to endure and overcome it.

To follow Christ, faithfully and unreservedly, is to follow a collision course with the world—that form and order of things opposed to God's will. There is a fundamental discord between the Christian and the world. The same spirit which crucified Christ will oppose, belittle, and persecute those who are His. We will face trials similar to those by which the Lord's foes tried to pollute His purity and dilute His devotion to the Father. He overcame all temptations, disdained all compromises, and never turned a fraction from His course. The world tried to turn Him aside by flattery and by threats, by trying to put Him on a throne and by actually succeeding in putting Him on a cross, but His purpose to do the Father's will remained steadfast.

Having conquered the world of the flesh, Christ came to Paul—and comes to us—saying, "My victory is yours." As He gave Himself *for* us, He gives himself *to* us, and through Him we are more than conquerors. We may bear in the body His dying, share His sufferings, but His life is manifested in us, too. The life of the self is crucified so that our lives may show forth *His* life. Thus we reach the summit meaning of life!

# 10

## THE ENDURANCE OF TRUE FAITH

*2 Cor. 4:11–18*
**11** For we who live are always delivered to death for Jesus' sake, that the life of Jesus may also be manifested in our mortal flesh. **12** So then death is working in us, but life in you. **13** But since we have the same spirit of faith, according to what is written, "I believed and therefore I spoke," we also believe and therefore speak, **14** knowing that He who raised up the Lord Jesus will also raise us up by Jesus, and will present us with you. **15** For all things are for your sakes, that grace, having spread through the many, may cause thanksgiving to abound to the glory of God. **16** Therefore we do not lose heart. But though our outward man is perishing, yet the inward man is being renewed day by day. **17** For our light affliction, which is but for a moment, is working for us a far more exceeding and eternal weight of glory, **18** while we do not look at the things which are seen, but at the things which are not seen. For the things which are seen are temporary, but the things which are not seen are eternal.

Verse 11 lends added emphasis to Paul's statement in the preceding verse, but here he also claimed that what he endured was for Jesus' sake. At his conversion he was commissioned to suffer for his Lord. The Lord said to Ananias of Damascus, concerning Paul, "I will show him what great things he must suffer for My name's sake" (Acts 9:16). Having understood and accepted that, Paul acknowledged that he took "pleasure in infirmities, in reproaches, in needs, in persecutions, in distresses, for Christ's sake" (2 Cor. 12:10). He could profess such willingness even though he knew that the path laid out for him was a death route (12:12)—one he would follow for Jesus' sake, supremely, but for the Corinthians and other churches as well.

## FAITH-LIVING

Such self-abnegation was not pious posturing or self-pity. Paul's faith, as expressed in verse 13, was drawn from his understanding and love of the Scriptures. He quoted Psalm 116:10, the testimony of an ancient saint, who endured great sorrow and affliction but was sustained by God: "I believed and therefore I spoke." That same spirit of faith was the dynamic for Paul's life, work, and suffering—and for the courage and confidence with which he spoke.

Another sustaining strength for Paul was his certainty of the triumphant resurrection of believers (v. 14). He put forth this lovely truth when he wrote that he and the Corinthians—and, by implication, we—will be raised up and presented faultless before the presence of God. It is a breathtaking prospect that those who are in Christ will be raised up *with* Him and presented *to* Him! Paul considered the triumphant resurrection of believers, the trophies and full fruition of Christ's death and resurrection, to be the glorious climax of God's redemptive purpose. At that time the blessed promise will be fulfilled: ". . . We shall be like Him, for we shall see Him as He is" (1 John 3:2).

There is a fine and valiant spirit evident in verse 15, where Paul wrote, "For all things are for your sakes, that [God's] grace, having spread through the many, may cause thanksgiving to abound to the glory of God." The first section of this verse is often considered apart from its contextual meaning and taken to mean that all that happens to the believer is for his benefit. I do not dispute—rather I rejoice in the fact that all that happens to the believer (within the will of God, of course) is for his benefit. But that is not what Paul was saying here. Instead, he declared that his ministry, his suffering, was for the Corinthians' sake, so that the grace of God might not be limited and localized but shed abroad by many, filling hearts with thanksgiving to God's glory.

## THE INNER RENEWAL

"Therefore," Paul continued in verse 16, "we do not lose heart." Paul was aware that death was working in him. The rigors of labor and suffering necessarily took their toll of the physical person. The body, wearied by stresses such as prison, travel, shipwreck, hunger, cold, and anxiety, was inevitably wasting away. At the same time, the inward person was being restored, renewed—and even growing stronger—through fellowship with Christ. A mystical, wondrous dichotomy was formed, the dying body synchronous with the thriving, joyous inner person!

We should not be careless about the health of our "inner person." This essential nature in us is not merely the part of us which is capable of knowledge, feeling, and will; it is the new, *spiritual* creation, new in *Christ,* as is so blessedly stated in 5:17 of this epistle. Born of the Spirit of God, our inner selves partake of the divine nature. The genius of Christian life and service is to give this new, spiritual person, indwelt and energized as it is by the Holy Spirit, dominance in our choice of action. The frustration many experience in attempting to live for and serve God is due to the fact that they are bound by the old nature, which is not capable of pleasing God, and ignore the "new creation" which is a delight to His eye.

Note Paul's words in verse 17 where he wrote of "our light affliction. . . ." What a valorous dismissal of the adversities he endured for his Lord and the church! Loneliness, misunderstanding, homelessness, physical frailty, buffeting by Satan (as all who stand bravely for Christ must expect), imprisonment—all this, and more, was a "light affliction"! Why? Because it was borne for Christ and His church. And because, balanced by the eternal blessings in Christ, it *was* light. Given this comparison, just imagine what the coming glory will be!

## THE "FAR LOOK"

Paul had the "far look," not in the sense that he was unconcerned with his responsibilities to his generation, but because he recognized the ultimate value of life by its eternal consequences. Beyond the toils of the road, the sojourn in a cold world, the lonely and perilous isolation which is often the lot of the godly soul, he saw the glory which awaited him. Like Moses, he "esteem [ed] the reproach of Christ greater riches . . . for he looked to the reward" (Heb. 11:26).

Jesus our Lord, ". . . for the joy that was set before Him endured the cross, despising the shame . . ." (Heb. 12:2) which He endured. And He teaches us that we belittle our faith when we consider it as a means of escaping the rigors of life. We lose the luster of it when we fail to see that the divine plan is to shape us, in the crucible, according to His image.

# 11

## PILGRIM IDENTITY, HEAVENLY CITIZENSHIP

*2 Cor. 5:1–8*

**1** For we know that if our earthly house, this tent, is destroyed, we have a building from God, a house not made with hands, eternal in the heavens. **2** For in this we groan, earnestly desiring to be clothed with our habitation which is from heaven, **3** if indeed, having been clothed, we shall not be found naked. **4** For we who are in this tent groan, being burdened, not because we want to be unclothed, but further clothed, that mortality may be swallowed up by life. **5** Now He who has prepared us for this very thing is God, who also has given us the Spirit as a deposit. **6** Therefore we are always confident, knowing that while we are at home in the body we are absent from the Lord. **7** For we walk in faith, not by sight. **8** We are confident, I say, and well-pleased rather to be absent from the body and to be present with the Lord.

Many speculations, questions, and opinions, some of them absurd, have been put forth concerning the transition from the mortal body to the immortal. This passage contains Paul's vital teaching about this matter, teaching couched in very positive terms. He began with the affirmation, "For we *know* . . . we have a building from God, a house not made with hands. . . ." The question has been raised why Paul used a conditional phrase here: "*if* our earthly house, this tent, is destroyed. . . ." Was it because he lived with the belief that Christ would (could, at least) return before he died? Or was he using "if" in the sense in which we often use it, meaning "even though"? The apostle did not clarify whether he expected to live to see his Lord's return, but he did intimate this anticipation at times.

## RESURRECTION ASSURANCE

In any case, Paul's position on what happens to the believer after physical death is clear. The tent of our earthly pilgrimage will be replaced with a building, a house made by God, eternal as its Maker is eternal, bearing the evidence of His divine skill. Paul did not belittle the body; rather, he exalted it as the temple of the Holy Spirit. But as the tabernacle, a tent, was replaced with a magnificent building, the temple, so these bodies are to be replaced with glorified, spiritual, incorruptible, eternal bodies, "conformed to His glorious body" (Phil. 3:21), fitted for the lofty life beyond. Presently we are pilgrims, in tents designed for camping or nomadic living. That pilgrim identity must be recognized, as well as our heavenly citizenship, which we will one day fully assume.

Twice in the passage Paul wrote "we groan" with desire to make the transition from tent to heavenly habitation. "We have a building" ready for us now, but it is not yet time to occupy it. So glorious, so superior to this earthly body (wonderful as *that* is) is that heavenly domicile that Paul was filled with longing to receive and occupy it.

Some commentators suggest that Paul's anxiety was generated by the thought of existing between death and resurrection without a body—an ethereal, incorporeal condition. Such an idea indicates a nakedness of identity repugnant to the Jewish mind. Holding this opinion, however, is tantamount to claiming that the great apostle's revelation from God was inadequate, and that he still clung to superstitions discredited by the new covenant. No doubt he wished to be changed from mortal flesh to the new, spiritual body without going through physical death. So would we all. It would be an experience of rapture, especially in view of the promise that the spiritual body we shall receive will be like that of Christ (1 Cor. 15:49; Phil. 3:21).

Paul, as has been previously noted, had a tendency to switch metaphors. Here, and in the following verses, he oscillated in describing man's condition between the idea of a house and that of a garment. The basic truth still is clear: "Mortality . . . swallowed up by life [or "absorbed by life" ]" is the Christian's blessed prospect. God has prepared us for this transformation (v. 5). He has given us a new nature, made us new creations, and "also has given us the [Holy] Spirit as a deposit [a guarantee of what is to follow ]." It is interesting to note that the word here translated "deposit" is used in modern Greek for "engagement ring." As the ring is given to seal the promise of marriage, God has given us His Spirit, by which we are "sealed for the day of redemption."

## IN THE HEAVENLIES

The beautiful words of Philippians 1:6 assure us that "He who has begun a good work in [us] will complete it until the day of Jesus Christ." And beyond that day, He has prepared us to enter and enjoy that life which is so far greater than we can now imagine. "Therefore," Paul wrote, "we are always confident [of good courage ]." Even though in this body we are "absent from the Lord," the apostle taught that we are in Christ, and He in us. As the body of Christ, we are joined to Him as our head. To appreciate fully what this means we must acknowledge the limitations of our present, physical life. Now "we see in a mirror, dimly" and "know in part," wrote Paul in 1 Corinthians 13:12. "We walk in faith, not by sight," while we are enveloped in these present bodies. We would rather be "absent from the body and [consequently ] to be present with the Lord."

From what Paul said here, as well as in such Scriptures as Philippians 1:23, we may believe the Christian goes directly, at death, to be with the Lord. The physical body is in the grave, or elsewhere, but the redeemed *person* is with Christ. In this connection, we may consider a question frequently asked: "How can a body which has been burned to ashes, or devoured by beasts, or in some other way scattered to the wind or by the sea, be raised, reassembled, and recognized?" Paul answered this question, saying that even though the physical body "is *destroyed,* we *have* a building . . . ," an eternal body. It is not a reconstructed version of the *tent* in which we now dwell, but a divinely made *house,* "eternal in the heavens."

# 12

## PRESENT GRACE
## AND FUTURE GLORY

*2 Cor. 5:9–16*

**9** Therefore we make it our aim, whether present or absent, to be well-pleasing to Him. **10** For we must all appear before the judgment seat of Christ, that each one may receive the things done in his body, according to what he has done, whether it is good or bad. **11** Knowing, therefore, the terror of the Lord, we persuade men; but we are well-known to God, and I also trust are well-known in your consciences. **12** For we do not commend ourselves again to you, but give you opportunity to glory on our behalf, that you may have something to answer those who glory in appearance and not in heart. **13** For if we are beside ourselves, it is for God; or if we are of sound mind, it is for you. **14** For the love of Christ constrains us, because we judge thus: that if One died for all, then all died; **15** and He died for all, that those who live should no longer live for themselves, but for Him who died for them and rose again. **16** Therefore, from now on, we know no one according to the flesh. Even though we have known Christ according to the flesh, yet now we know Him thus no longer.

Of the twenty-one verses of chapter 5, nine of them begin with the word "for" and six with the word "therefore" (NKJV–NT). The continuity of Paul's thought is thus markedly evident. Verses may be considered separately for devotional or illustrative purposes, but full comprehension of the chapter is possible only when they are read together as grammatically and doctrinally inseparable. When doing so, it is helpful to follow this rule: with each "therefore" determine what it is *there* for (admittedly not good grammar, but proper practice nevertheless). Verse 9, for instance, begins with a "therefore"; its purpose is to continue the thought of preceding verses, especially verses 6–8 in which Paul spoke of being present in or absent from the body and absent from or present with the Lord. In this verse he emphasized that, whatever the case, wherever he was—in the body or with the Lord—his highest aim was to be "well-pleasing to Him."

Present grace and future glory are not to be considered indifferently. Indeed, the quality, if not the validity, of our Christian profession may well be judged by the degree to which we live in a manner which is "well-pleasing to Him." And having pleased Him, having gained the supreme commendation, satisfying humans loses significance. Eadie puts it beautifully: "The *presence* of Christ is the cheer of my life; the *Spirit* of Christ the life of my life; the *love* of Christ the power of my life, the *will* of Christ the law of my life; the *glory* of Christ the end of my life."*

## THE JUDGMENT OF THE BELIEVER'S WORKS

An important factor in Paul's living and ministry was his awareness of the fact that "we must all appear before the judgment seat of Christ." This judgment is not to be a universal one, for both Christians and non-Christians, but instead specifically a time when the believer's "work will become manifest" (1 Cor. 3:13). The Christian's sins were judged *in* Christ—He died for those sins—but the Christian's works will be judged *by* Christ. There are ethical, moral considerations here. We should be required to answer for, to be rewarded or to forfeit rewards for, what we have done with God's gift of grace in His Son, Jesus Christ. A slogan I carry in my Bible says, "Your life is God's gift to you. What you do with it is your gift to God." The quality of our present will be manifest at the "Bema," the judgment seat of Christ.

---

*\*Abingdon Bible Commentary* (Nashville, Tenn.: Abingdon Press, 1929), p. 1243.

The word "appear" in verse 10 is more accurately translated "manifested" or "be made manifest." Whatever else will be evident at that final time, God's grace will be more clearly seen than is possible now. We shall see, surely, how unworthy we have been and, in spite of that unworthiness, how faithfully, graciously, and lovingly He has kept us, led us, spared us! We "know in part," now, what God's grace is; then we shall finally, truly, comprehend the magnitude and marvel of it!

An enormous disparity of opinion exists concerning the word "terror" in verse 11, with the translation throughout the New Testament being almost unanimously "fear." The thought of God as the judge of unbelieving, unrepentant, rebellious sinners may well bring terror, eventually, to them. This particular passage, however, is not concerned with this emotion. Instead Paul's meaning was probably: "Motivated by the fear of the Lord [in the sense of reverential awe, and the fear that we do not please Him] we persuade men." The apostle manifested great urgency here, as he did in verse 20. There he spoke of "God . . . pleading by us" while he "implores . . . in Christ's behalf. . . ."

Paul gained comfort and confidence in God's knowledge of his heart and approval of his labors. He felt no need to defend himself to his Lord, to whom he was already "well-known."

Such support was supremely important as a credential for his ministry, but Paul continued to hope that the Christian conscience of the Corinthians would approve and support that ministry. He emphasized that the spirit in which he wrote was not self-defense or personal commendation. Several times in the epistle (4:2;6:4) he did indeed speak of commending himself, but here he clearly stated the contrary. His purpose here was to suggest an answer which the Corinthians might use in response to Paul's opponents. If you wish to judge me or to defend me, to condemn me or to boast of me, wrote the apostle, let truth be the basis of what you say.

The enemies of Paul spoke of him as eccentric, erratic, even mad. Paul would not deny that he had had ecstatic experiences, but he did not flaunt them; they were between himself and God. What he communicated to people was not of that nature; he spoke and wrote in truth and sobriety, and he asked the Corinthians to recognize that fact.

## THE CONSTRAINT OF LOVE

It was Christ's love which "constrained" (sometimes translated "controlled" or "compelled") Paul and motivated his service. Christ's love led Him to the cross, and in His death we all died. "I have been crucified with Christ," wrote the apostle in Galatians 2:20. But in that death the Christian also gains the right to participate and be raised to new, eternal life in Him. That new life, according to verse 15, is ours, not to be lived for self, but for Him whose death and resurrection paid for and secured it. Here is indicated the level of life on which we are to live, and here is provided a test by which we may know whether or not we are "well-pleasing to Him."

Paul abandoned and renounced life on the level of the flesh. At one time he (and we) knew Christ with human knowledge and recognition. Now that we can know Him as Savior and Lord, our life, our joy, our choice of priorities should be clear.

# 13

## NEW CREATURES IN CHRIST

2 Cor. 5:17
**17** Therefore, if anyone is in Christ, he is a new creation;
old things have passed away; behold, all things have become
new.

The seventeenth verse of chaper 5 is of great significance and
dearly loved. It is often quoted, though usually apart from its
context in which Paul described the transformation following
faith in Christ. But here he sets forth the conclusion and climax
of his thoughts, that this transformation is so radical as to bring
about a new creation. "Therefore," wrote the apostle, alluding
to what he said in preceding verses, "if anyone is in Christ, he is
a new creation." In this statement two phrases stand out as
extraordinarily important: "in Christ" and "new creation,"
both of which deserve more emphasis than they usually receive
in contemporary preaching and teaching.

### PAUL'S FAVORITE PHRASE

The phrase "in Christ," or its equivalent, such as "in Him"
or "in whom," was used frequently—more than 160 times—by
Paul. Eminent scholars consider it to be his most characteristic
and favorite phrase. Its implications are extensive but summed
up in the fact that the believer is in such union with Christ that
he has been crucified, resurrected, and then given the power to
ascend with Him, *in* Him.

Consider the blessed dichotomy: We are in Christ, and *He* is
in us. He is the vine; we are the branches. His life becomes ours
by this sublime union. What certainty and security it brings, to
know that we live in Him, and He in us! To recognize that we

are in Christ, *truly* to believe it, takes away forever the slavish and frightening notion that our salvation is tentative, unstable. A dying old saint, asked if she were not fearful that, even now, she might "slip through God's fingers and be lost," answered, "That cannot be. I *am* one of His fingers."

The blessed recognition of our being in Christ gives the believer a true sense and demonstration of sanctification. Christ is living His life in us, wrote Paul in his great affirmation in Galatians 2:20. *His* life, *His* Spirit, *His* holiness, *His* love—it is all *His* in us by grace.

## ENTIRELY NEW

The second phrase, "a new creation," also merits more attention than it usually receives. We do not receive Christ as Savior and Lord and then do the best we can with our innate resources to live creditably as Christians. Instead we become, at conversion, a *new creation*—new in the sense of being a *new, different order.*

David recognized this transformation in his penitential Psalm (51) by appealing to God: "Create in me a clean heart, O God. . . ." And each of us, made to see his sin and need apart from the transforming grace of God, must echo the cry of the psalmist king. If we are to be cleansed and made righteous, it must be by His creative power, His ability to make something new from us. "For we are His workmanship [or, handiwork], created in Christ Jesus . . ." (Eph. 2:30).

## PRESENCE AND POWER

Some people will advise you, "Discover that person within you, that superior personality just waiting to be loosed." But the *Scripture* says, in many and various ways, "Beware that person within you!" (Even Freud said that. He found, down deep in humanity, a sinister capability for incredible wickedness and selfishness.) Unable to free ourselves from the toils of flesh, we need someone above us to come and live in us and through us, bringing power and purpose, purity and peace, to life. Christ is that someone whose presence and power can bring to us a new nature. While on this earth, though, this new creation in our hearts may not always be manifest. The most dedicated, most fully committed Christian is at times disappointed in his actions, thoughts, moods, and reactions. This disappointment should be a cause of joy since it is a confirmation of the wondrous change taking place in his life. Before his conversion inappropriate actions would have been of little concern, while as a new creation, partaking of the divine nature, he views them with feelings appropriate to that new nature.

Once transformed we have no room for "the old things." The dominion of sin and the congenital tendency to transgress God's law, will, and love have passed away. In their place, "the new has come." Of course, we are not to suppose that since "old things have passed away," we are no longer subject to temptation or responsible for exercising our wills on the side of God and righteousness. The Bible never dismisses the power of the tempter as trivial, instead speaking of him as "the prince of the power of the air," "the god of this age," of fearful power and malevolence. Victory over him is not automatic. At the same time, we are assured of victory as we "walk in the Spirit" (Gal. 5:16). Numerous admonitions are found in Scripture, calling us to appropriate the new and wonderful provisions which God has made for our spiritual strength and overcoming grace.

# 14

## RECONCILIATION

*2 Cor. 5:18–21*

**18** And all things are of God, who has reconciled us to Himself through Jesus Christ, and has given us the ministry of reconciliation, **19** That is, that God was in Christ reconciling the world to Himself, not imputing their trespasses to them, and has committed to us the word of reconciliation. **20** Therefore we are ambassadors for Christ, as though God were pleading by us: we implore you in Christ's behalf, be reconciled to God. **21** For He has made Him who knew no sin to be sin for us, that we might become the righteousness of God in Him.

Here Paul took up the subject—one not very generously considered by many teachers of theology—of reconciliation. It is a profoundly important matter, worthy of our careful attention, and one which should inspire reverent gratitude as we explore its implications.

## IT ALL BEGAN WITH GOD

The first point, as is evident throughout this passage, is that reconciliation began with God. Verse 18 begins by proclaiming, "And all things are of God. . . ." That is, the redeeming, transforming wonders wrought by Christ had their inception in the mind and will and love of God. It was He who "reconciled us to Himself through Jesus Christ," and He who has "given us the ministry of reconciliation."

Some theologians once taught—as some may still do— that God the Father had only punishment of sinners in mind, and that God the Son persuaded Him to spare them, offering Himself as the sacrifice for their sins. One wonders how such ideas could exist in any spiritually enlightened mind. There is massive evidence in Scripture that the Father *sent* the Son to earth to save us. "God so loved the world that He gave His only begotten Son . . ." (John 3:16), said Jesus. And here Paul wrote: ". . . God was *in* Christ reconciling the world to Himself. . . ." Thus the Father gave His Son (John 3:16), and the Son gave Himself (1 John 3:16).

## AN ALL-IMPORTANT DISTINCTION

The distinction should be kept carefully in mind, too, that it was *man* who needed to be reconciled to *God*, not God to man. Numerous figures are used in Scripture to depict the human state apart from God. As lost sheep and aimless prodigals, we are described as spiritually dead, blind and unclean, proud and vain. And surely, as P. T. Forsyth points out, we are revealed to be rebels against God, alienated and estranged from Him by our fallen nature.*

This alienation is hard for some Christian preachers and teachers to accept. As God's children, they profess, even at our sorry, sinful worst, none of us will be permitted to be lost by a love so great as His. That love *has* provided redemption and reconciliation, but God has released to us the privilege of accepting it, or the responsibility of refusing it. We alone can not *effect* the reconciliation to God because we are not capable of such a spiritual action. All that we can do to end that alienation is to exercise the faith He bestowed upon us to believe in and receive salvation, for this is the only course of action of which we are capable which ends in fellowship with God. Following that path, however, is a journey many refuse to undertake, and they remain estranged from Him.

The great wonder of Christ's sacrifice is that, having believed

---

*Positive Preaching and the Modern Mind* (Grand Rapids, Mich.: Baker, 1980), p. 38.

in Christ, our trespasses are not imputed to (counted against) us, but to Him. This truth, expressed in verse 19, is amplified in breathtaking terms in verse 21. Christ was "made . . . sin for us, that we might become the righteousness of God in Him." Thus He cried on the cross, "My God, my God, why have You forsaken me?" He endured God's wrath, not against man, *surely* not against Himself, but against sin, so that sin might never be counted against any who believe in Christ. It should be admitted that we cannot fully comprehend Christ being "made sin for us" or our becoming "the righteousness of God in Him." We find ourselves incapable of explaining—even of understanding—these principles in any adequate sense. But our redeemed, reconciled spirits are enabled by God's grace to appropriate them—even half comprehended—and, consequently, to rejoice in them with joy unspeakable.

## OUR INDISPENSABLE DUTY

Twice in the passage Paul said that the ministry, or the word, of reconciliation has been committed to those of us reconciled to God. One who has experienced salvation naturally and properly concerns himself with the salvation of others. He recognizes sharing the treasure of grace which he has received as the way to become a representative, or ambassador, of his Lord and Savior.

This path of transition is one many professed Christians do not understand or want to follow. The proclamation of God's love and grace is perceived by them to be the responsibility of a select group especially qualified for such a ministry. One of their excuses for silence is the claim that they have no gifts which enable them to witness for Christ. Withdrawal may be disguised behind such a statement as: "My Christian faith is a very personal, very private matter. I do not feel inclined to talk about it to others." Such refusal to share is not only contrary to biblical instruction, it runs counter to our natural inclinations.

When a happy event happens to us, we want to tell someone as soon as possible. Our joys are heightened and enriched as we tell others. Surely, then, our reconciliation to God is made sweeter when we urge others: "Be reconciled to God."

# 15

# THE MARKS OF THE MAN OF GOD

*2 Cor. 6:1–10*
1 We then, as workers together with Him, plead with you also that you not receive the grace of God in vain. 2 For He says: "I have heard you in an accepted time, And in the day of salvation I have helped you." Behold, now is the accepted time; behold, now is the day of salvation. 3 We give no offense in anything, that our ministry not be blamed. 4 But in all things we commend ourselves as ministers of God: in much patience, in tribulations, in needs, in distresses, 5 in stripes, in imprisonments, in tumults, in labors, in sleeplessness, in fastings; 6 by purity, by knowledge, by longsuffering, by kindness, by the Holy Spirit, by unfeigned love, 7 by the word of truth, by the power of God, by the armor of righteousness on the right hand and on the left, 8 by honor and dishonor, by evil report and good report; as deceivers, and yet true; 9 as unknown, and yet well-known; as dying, and behold we live; as chastened, and yet not killed; 10 as sorrowful, yet always rejoicing; as poor, yet making many rich; as having nothing, and yet possessing all things.

In the closing verses of chapter 5 Paul wrote of the ministry of reconciliation which had been committed to him and to others. Those so commissioned he called "ambassadors for Christ," as though God were appealing to men by them. That appeal they voice is this: "Be reconciled to God." Further estrangement is needless and indefensible, for Christ has taken our sin that we might become righteous before God with our sins no longer counted against us.

I feel that the apostle, having introduced the subject of God's redeeming love and Christ's sacrificial offering, felt constrained to give it a brief but urgent emphasis. "We then, as workers together ["with Him" is not in the original but is felt by many scholars to be implied; it is my opinion that, though other Scriptures clearly identify us as God's fellow-workers, Paul was speaking here of his fellow ministers] plead with you also that you not receive the grace of God in vain."

## THE ESSENTIAL FOR SALVATION

Paul then quoted the familiar words of Isaiah 49:8, an oft-used evangelistic text: "Behold, now is the accepted time; behold, now is the day of salvation." He has already indicated that he is writing to believers, having addressed them in his greetings of the first chapter as "the church of God . . . with all the saints. . . ." Why, then, this appeal not to receive the grace of God in vain, and this reminder that salvation is offered *now,* with the implied warning that later may be too late?

Probably some members of the Corinthian and Achaian assemblies were *with* the church and *with* the saints, but not *of* them. We know ourselves how some people choose the company of Christians but are never personally reconciled to God. It was not and is not enough to be identified with the *church;* a personal faith in *Christ* as Savior, and acceptance of Him as Lord, is essential to salvation.

## GOD'S GRACE AND OUR DEMONSTRATION OF IT

If this is the primary purpose and meaning of Paul's appeal, as I believe it is, other implications can also be drawn. It is surely true that every believer, in some measure, fails to make effective use of God's gift of grace and, therefore, receives that grace, in a sense, in vain. God's provisions for us are enormously greater than our appropriations of them. Our *knowledge* of grace greatly exceeds our *demonstration* of it. Many of us spend our time in the suburbs of doctrinal orthodoxy, missing the fulfillment found at the center of God's will. A Christian should constantly ask of himself: "How much of God's grace to me is without effect in my life?"

Paul's appeal is compelling, since it voices God's appeal to us, but its acceptance by the Corinthians was supported by the indispensable factor of his own blameless life and Christian character. Those who rejected God's grace among the Corinthians could take no refuge behind any delinquency or deficiency on Paul's part. They were thus denied a common excuse for indifference toward, or rejection of, the claims of Christ: the picking of flaws, whether actual or imagined, in the lives of believers, especially ministers. Paul and his fellow ministers could face such charges with this statement: "We give no offense in anything" or "we put no obstacle in anyone's way." ". . . But in all things we commend ourselves as ministers of God. . . ."

## THE "ALL THINGS" WORTHY
## OF COMMENDATION

What were these "all things" mentioned in verse 4 for which such commendation was deserved? Modern ministers are often commended for their excellence in preaching, their administrative skills, effectiveness in securing funds for the church, and other desirable qualities. Such achievements seldom enter the sphere in which Paul ministered commendably: "in much patience [or, endurance], in tribulations [afflictions], in needs [hardships], in distresses [calamities], in stripes [beatings], in imprisonments, in tumults, in labors, in fastings [hunger]." Many ministers today, subjected to such experiences, would feel totally rejected and ineffectual, even worthless! We owe an enormous debt to Paul, not only for what he wrote but for what he was and what he suffered for his and our Lord. His tribulations poignantly remind us what it means to be "always carrying about in the body the dying of the Lord Jesus . . ." (4:10), and be "always delivered to death for Jesus' sake . . ." (4:11).

However, unlikely it may be that we may be called upon to endure such arduous experiences, we should be so fully and wholeheartedly committed and consecrated to our Lord that we can say, from our deepest hearts,

> "Jesus, I my cross have taken,
> All to leave and follow Thee;
> Destitute, despised, forsaken
> Thou, from hence, my all shalt be."

—Henry F. Lyte, 1793–1847

## BY THE HOLY SPIRIT'S ENABLING

The apostle commended himself as a minister of God not only by his brave acceptance of hardship and suffering, which is developed more fully in chapter 11, but by positive personal graces and practices. A picture of integrity, godliness, and spiritual perception is painted, which reveals Paul as the classic and ideal minister.

The first characteristic Paul mentioned was "purity," by which he meant not only moral rectitude and chastity but honorable thoughts and actions in all areas of life. "Knowledge" refers to general understanding, and even more specifically to insight and understanding according to the Spirit— the capacity to grasp divine truth. "Longsuffering" (or "forbearance," as preferred by some translators) is the quality of patient toleration of others' unpleasantness, and "kindness" is the spirit of aggressive good will.

The question has been raised whether the translation of "by the Holy Spirit" should not instead be "by the spirit of holiness," since Paul was listing personal graces and qualifications. The position taken in these studies is that the apostle was inserting a reminder that all he was and all he did was dependent upon, and confirmed by, the Holy Spirit.

Paul's "unfeigned (or "genuine") love" certainly did commend his ministry, and such love is essential on the part of anyone seeking to serve God and man. The lack of this quality, as 1 Corinthians 13:2 emphasizes, reduces any ministry, any sacrifice, any gift, however remarkable, to nothing. The apostle not only enjoined this *agape* love upon others, he stated that it was a basic motive and the spirit of his own ministry.

## OBEDIENCE TO THE WORD

"By the word of truth" is thought by some to imply simply "truthful speech," but given the immediate context it seems evident that Paul had in mind the divine truth of the gospel. Another possibility is the idea that a truth may be stated in such a way as to convey untruth. Elsewhere (4:2) Paul wrote of "handling the word of God deceitfully" (or tampering with God's Word).

Paul's ministry always relied upon "the power of God" and was always protected by "the armor of righteousness" (v. 7). He recognized his total dependence upon God's power, at the same time realizing that this power could be released only in a life which was righteous—i.e., obedient to God's Word and conformed to God's will. No ministry can be truly effective unless it issues from righteous living.

## COUNTING THE COST

Paul closed this passage with a brief allusion to the consequences of his ministry. He had received "honor" at times and endured "dishonor" at other times. As he told the Philippians, he had learned "how to be abased" and "how to abound," "to be full and to be hungry." He acknowledged that following Christ cost him certain social, political, and ecclesiastical rights and privileges, but he gladly "suffered the loss of all things . . . that he might gain Christ" (Phil. 3:8) by serving as His minister and apostle.

The apostle also came to know the meaning of what F. W. Farrar, in an apt phrase, calls "the beatitude of malediction": "Blessed are you when men hate you,/And when they exclude

you,/And revile you, and cast out your name as evil,/For the
Son of Man's sake" (Luke 6:22). "If you are reproached for the
name of Christ, blessed are you . . ." (1 Pet. 4:14). Whatever
lies might have been spoken against him by enemies of Christ,
Paul nevertheless was honored by those who were friends of our
Lord and, certainly, by the Lord Himself.

This honor, coming as a blessing from God for his obedience,
turned situations most of us would consider dreadful into
victories for God's glory. Paul, for instance, was accused, as his
Lord was (John 7:12), of being a deceiver, but his message and
his life repudiated the charge. He was dismissed as being
"unknown" but, here again, what he was and did disproved the
slur. He admitted that he was "dying" (4:16), but only in so far
as the outward man was concerned for the inward man was
thriving and joyous. He was "chastened," as all of God's
children are and must be at times, "but not killed." God's
chastenings are always beneficial since they certify our sonship
to Him (Heb. 12:7); they make us "partakers of His holiness"
(Heb. 12:10), and develop in us the righteousness which He
desires (Heb. 12:11). Profane and carnal minds may perceive
chastening as proof of *rejection* by God; the devout soul accepts
it as evidence of His *love.*

Verse 10 completes and climaxes the succession of contrasts
outlined above. Paul wrote of being "sorrowful," "poor," "having nothing," yet "always rejoicing," "making many rich,"
"possessing all things." These are paradoxes incomprehensible
to minds and hearts where Christ does not dwell and rule. Such
trauma, for those unacquainted with the cheering, enriching
presence of Christ, seem inconsolable misery. But to those
whose hearts are His, there is joy which triumphs over sorrow,
and spiritual wealth which far transcends the decaying riches of
earth.

# 16

## PAUL'S APPEAL FOR
## LARGENESS OF HEART

*2 Cor. 6:11–13*
**11** O Corinthians! We have spoken openly to you, our heart is wide open. **12** You are not restricted by us, but you are restricted by your own affections. **13** Now in return for the same (I speak as to children), you also be open.

The apostle Paul, misunderstood and, at least in some measure, mistreated by the Corinthians, took the initiative in restoring strong and loving relations between himself and this church. We should be inspired by the affectionate appeals for mutual love, written in the face of adversity, with which the apostle filled the Second Epistle to the Corinthians. Paul's feelings were intense, especially as seen in verse 11 where he exclaimed, "O Corinthians!" This is the only example, in either of his letters, in which he addressed them by name, outside of the salutations. Such emotion was coupled with a reminder that he had spoken frankly to them in preceding passages, affirming the reasonableness of his actions and the worthiness of his message. His words of caring flew from a heart which was "wide open," or, as the original King James version puts it, "enlarged."

## THE BENCHMARK FOR
## CHRISTIAN COMMUNICATION

In Paul's words here we find a benchmark for communication between Christians in cases of misunderstanding. Plainness of speech is necessary. Frequently the problem has arisen because of a lack of honest, candid expression. But plainness of speech alone may compound the difficulty unless it issues from that vital attitude, largeness of heart. One may be correct in assessing a situation but neutralize the worth of this judgment by the manner and spirit of expression. Nowhere in Paul's discussion of the Corinthian problems does this largeness of heart fail him, even though he cannot conceal his anguish.

One wonders how many dissensions and estrangements in the church might be avoided if largeness of heart helped temper plainness of speech. Too often the clamorous voice of self gains our attention, rather than the quiet, reasonable, and loving Spirit of God. Resulting from this imbalance are broken fellowship, ruptured friendships, and forfeited respect for the cause of Christ on the part of the onlooking world.

## RESTORATION THROUGH LOVE

In this passage it is evident that reconciliation has taken place between the apostle and the Corinthians—or, more properly, between Paul and that element in the Corinthian church which had been opposed and rebellious toward Paul. Still something was lacking. Paul diagnosed a restraint on the part of the Corinthians and a failure to return the affection he felt and expressed. "If barriers exist," he said in essence, "they are in your hearts, not mine. I have opened my mouth to you and my heart to you. Please do the same to me." Paul knows that mere apologies and resumption of civilities is not sufficient restoration in the sacred body of Christ, the church. *Love* must be renewed, and every conscientious Christian will do whatever is necessary to effect that restoration.

The need for revival in the church—revival in the sense of quickened zeal, confessed and forsaken sin, and renewed devotion to the Word of God and the church of Christ—is rightfully stressed from the pulpit and acknowledged in the pew. An important aspect of any such revival, if it is geniune, are lateral as well as vertical results. We should realize that true revival will not only bring us back to God's blessing and fellowship; it will foster largeness of heart in the church. Away will be swept the critical, suspicious, and churlish spirit, and replacing it will be divine love. Those who have been thus filled with God's love will not stand aloof, allowing barriers to remain. Their initiative to restore peace and fellowship accepts the risk of rejection, in order "to keep the unity of the Spirit in the bond of peace" (Eph. 4:3).

# 17

## PAUL'S APPEAL FOR HOLINESS

*2 Cor. 6:14–7:1*
**14** Do not be unequally yoked together with unbelievers. For what fellowship has righteousness with lawlessness? And what communion has light with darkness? **15** And what accord has Christ with Belial? Or what part has he who believes with an unbeliever? **16** And what agreement has the temple of God with idols? For you are the temple of the living God. As God has said: "I will dwell in them/And walk among them./I will be their God,/And they shall be My people." **17** "Therefore come out from among them/And be separate, says the Lord./Do not touch what is unclean,/And I will receive you." **18** "I will be a Father to you,/And you shall be My sons and daughters,/Says the LORD Almighty."

**1** Therefore, having these promises, beloved, let us cleanse ourselves from all filthiness of the flesh and spirit, perfecting holiness in the fear of God.

These verses are considered a parenthesis by some writers, an interruption by others. A number have suggested that this passage was part of a "lost" letter Paul is said to have written to the Corinthians, that the loose papyrus sheets became detached and were wrongly replaced. My position is that the apostle was writing a letter, not organizing a treatise, about a subject which inspired deep emotions in him: the spiritual state of Christians dear to him. Naturally he would deal with the emotion and the varied concerns as they came to mind by making whatever transitions were necessary without regard to a formal structure.

### IN, BUT NOT OF, THE WORLD

Whatever may be said about the *location* of this passage, the *message* of it is crucially important: "Do not be unequally yoked together with unbelievers." This command has been voiced to God's people from the advent of their history. No fellowship with God is possible without separation from that which offends Him. Israel, for instance, was called into isolation from other peoples so that they might be one people under God and produce for the world God's Word, the Bible, and God's Son, the Savior. Christians are likewise called to recognize that they are in, but not of, the world. What fellowship has righteousness with lawlessness? What communion has light with darkness? What accord has Christ with Belial (not in the Old Testament a proper name, the word meant "worthlessness, wickedness," although here it seems to refer to Satan)? What communion has the believer with an unbeliever? What agreement has the temple of God with idols? Paul asked these rhetorical questions with one answer in mind: none. Christians are God's temple and are to consider themselves as such, sanctified (set apart) for His service and His glory.

This lesson of separation of believer and unbeliever is strongly and clearly put. However, the message of this passage has been twisted by some separatists to justify a sanctimonious detachment from other believers who truly serve Christ but who do not voice the same narrow shibboleths as do these groups. The erring Christians who misuse Paul's words should be reminded that he was speaking against union with *unbelievers*, not believers, and against lawlessness, satanic influence, and idols, not against those who accept and serve Christ as Savior and Lord.

## CONTACT, NOT COMPLICITY

The admonishment against union with an unbeliever is, furthermore, not an instruction to stand apart, in self-righteous aloofness, from those who are not yet Christians. *Contact* with them is unavoidable—indeed, it is necessary for social, congenial relations—but no *complicity* should be fostered which neutralizes the Christian's influence. We may—and should—unite with non-Christians in the quest for good government, civic welfare, and other common human concerns, but we are *never* to compromise, *never* to participate in anything incompatible with what God requires of us. Vigilance is needed to fulfill our mission to spread light, by God's grace, and to avoid entering into the darkness around us.

Paul's series of questions is followed by three quotations from the Old Testament—beautiful assertions by God, climaxed by the statement that, as men turn *from* evil to lives which are separated *to* Him, He becomes their Father. (The idea that God is the common father of men is fallacious; we *become* His children by spiritual birth, not by natural generation.) According to many readers, Paul did not transcribe accurately. If so, the errors were certainly caused by having no copies of those particular Scriptures at hand; however, the proper meaning *was* conveyed, which is, after all, the essence of any scriptural passage.

## PROGRESS IN HOLINESS

Chapter 7, verse 1, tells us that, having been given these promises (6:16–18), we are first of all to cleanse ourselves from (that is, put away) that which defiles either our bodies or our spirits. Only God can cleanse us from sin, but He has released to us the power to put away whatever has a defiling influence in our lives. We are not to attempt to do what only He can do, nor are we to expect Him to do what He has assigned to us, although He has promised His enabling grace to us in the doing of His will. We are called, not to a relative cleanliness in which we are mostly healed, but to a cleansing of ourselves from *all* defilement in both body and spirit. Boast of freedom from sensual sin is inadequate if, at the same time, we harbor terrible sins of the spirit.

The second action we are to take is the "perfecting holiness in the fear [reverent awe] of God." In other words, we should always work on bringing more completeness and maturity to our new lives in Christ. What we consecrate to God is made holy by that consecration, and true Christian living is the deepening of that consecration by ensuing obedience and commitment. Thus the soul grows into the likeness of Christ, as it is conformed to His image (Rom. 8:29).

# 18

## THE LANGUAGE OF
## CHRISTLIKE LOVE

2 Cor. 7:2–16

**2** Open your hearts to us. We have wronged no one, we have corrupted no one, we have defrauded no one. **3** I do not say this to condemn you; for I have said before that you are in our hearts, to die together and to live together. **4** Great is my boldness of speech toward you, great is my boasting on your behalf. I am filled with comfort. I am exceedingly joyful in all our tribulation. **5** For indeed, when we came to Macedonia, our flesh had no rest, but we were troubled on every side. Outside were conflicts, inside were fears. **6** Nevertheless God, who comforts the downcast, comforted us by the coming of Titus, **7** and not only by his coming, but also by the consolation with which he was comforted in you, when he told us your earnest desire, your mourning, your zeal for me, so that I rejoiced even more. **8** For though I made you sorry with my letter, I do not regret it; though I did regret it. For I perceive that the same epistle has made you sorry, though only for a while. **9** Now I rejoice, not that you were made sorry, but that your sorrow led to repentance. For you were made sorry in a godly manner, that you might suffer loss from us in nothing. **10** For godly sorrow produces repentance to salvation, not to be regretted; but the sorrow of the world produces death. **11** For observe this very thing, that you sorrowed in a godly manner: What diligence it produced in you, what clearing of yourselves, what indignation, what fear, what vehement desire, what zeal, what vindication! In all things you have proved yourselves to be clear in this matter. **12** Therefore, although I wrote to you, I did not do it for the sake of him who had done the wrong, nor for the sake of him who suffered wrong, but that our care for you in the sight of God might appear to you. **13** Therefore we have been comforted in your comfort. And we rejoiced exceed-

ingly more for the joy of Titus, because his spirit has been
refreshed by you all. **14** For if in anything I have boasted to
him about you, I am not ashamed. But as we spoke all things
to you in truth, even so our boasting to Titus was found true.
**15** And his affections are greater for you as he remembers the
obedience of you all, how with fear and trembling you
received him. **16** Therefore I rejoice that I have confidence
in you in everything.

Paul here resumed the outpouring of his personal feelings
concerning the estrangement and reconciliation with the
Corinthians. "Open your hearts to us. We have wronged . . .
corrupted . . . defrauded no one. . . ." This is the language of a
thoroughly upright, ethical, and Christian man. Painful as it is
to be misjudged, falsely accused, and rejected, the sting is
lessened by knowing in your heart that you are innocent. A bad
conscience embitters the sweetest comfort, but a good conscience sweetens the bitterest cross. Paul enjoyed the latter.

## RESTORATION

Often in asserting one's own blamelessness, others are condemned. Paul gently, sensitively avoided such a pitfall, assuring the Corinthians that no condemnation of them was intended. Paul was simply seeking for a Christian solution to a
bad situation. So far as the Corinthians were concerned, his
heart was one with theirs in love, not only in time and at death,
but in eternity.

The fourth verse of Chapter 7 is an outburst of confidence
and pride in the Corinthians, expressing the comfort and joy
that was Paul's even in the midst of his many trials. Paul knew
these sufferings were his lot, as he told the Ephesian elders in
that tender exhortation at Miletus: ". . . the Holy Spirit
testifies in every city, saying that chains and tribulations await
me" (Acts 20:23). We know already the problems he faced:
rebellious churches; his work threatened by Jewish, pagan, and

even Christian fanatics; personal depression; and fear—fear not only for himself but also for those who were in spiritual need and danger.

Still, heavy as these problems were, the restored relationship with the Corinthians gave him joy and strength. The coming of Titus, who was filled with joyous confidence and who brought good news of the change in the Corinthian church, would help Paul beat whatever trouble came to him. Titus, a trusted and treasured coworker with Paul, acted as Paul's representative to the Corinthians. Having been received by them with fear and trembling, as verse 15 indicates, he became aware, at last, of the seriousness of the condition into which they had fallen. Deeply moved and troubled, grief-stricken over their actions, they repented and were restored to spiritual blessing and peace.

## THE BLESSING OF GODLY SORROW

The essential validity of the Corinthians' Christianity was shown in the sorrow—and the *kind* of sorrow—they felt as the Holy Spirit (through Paul's letter and, no doubt, Titus' counsel and prayers) convicted them of their spiritual lapse. That letter of Paul's had been painful for him to write and for them to receive. Yet, though he regretted the necessity of it, the apostle rejoiced in its effect, for it brought a cleansing sorrow to them. This emotion of the Corinthians was far deeper than a feeling of regret over a wrong action or attitude; it was a sorrow toward God, producing repentance, divine forgiveness, and restoration. Sorrow alone can be self-centered, morbid, and despairing; sorrow "according to God"—the literal wording—leads to blessing.

The fates of Judas and Peter illustrate this difference in degree. Judas was remorseful over his betrayal of Jesus. Though seemingly frantic with that emotion he evinced no evidence of what is called here "godly sorrow," and he died in disgrace. Peter sorrowed, too—we are told that he "wept bitterly"—but his sorrow produced repentance and restoration. It is fascinating to see that, when God chose a spokesman on the day of Pentecost, His choice was Peter.

## THE NEED FOR TRUE REPENTANCE

The sincerity and intensity of the Corinthians' feelings could not be doubted: "What diligence . . . what clearing of yourselves, what indignation, what fear, what vehement desire. . . ." How wonderful it would be if there were more of such earnestness and concern today on the part of those who profess the grace of God. Many Christians seem little concerned about their own spiritual deficiencies, the state of the church, or the need of the world. No appeal is intended here for a return to the grim and forbidding kind of piety of some of our forefathers. It is a reasonable concern, however, that the jolly preaching and pop music in style in many places does not really stimulate Christians to strive for spiritual growth. We need to recognize superficiality and shallowness for what they really are. A joyous faith is a treasure, rightfully the possession of a true believer, but it must issue from a heart truly repentant of sin.

The chapter has a happy ending. Paul was comforted, as were the Corinthians. Titus rejoiced in the spiritual renewal of the church, and Paul gloried in the confidence he had in its members. The breach was healed.

# 19

## THE GRACE OF GIVING

*2 Cor. 8:1–5*

1 Moreover, brethren, we make known to you the grace of God bestowed on the churches of Macedonia: 2 that in a great trial of affliction the abundance of their joy and their deep poverty abounded to the riches of their liberality. 3 For I bear witness that according to their ability, yes, and beyond their ability, they were freely willing, 4 imploring us with much urgency that we would receive the gift and the fellowship of the ministering to the saints. 5 And this they did, not as we had hoped, but first gave themselves to the Lord, and then to us by the will of God.

The eighth chapter begins the second major division of this epistle. Here Paul developed some beautiful and important teachings concerning the grace of God manifested in giving. His immediate concern was the Christians in Jerusalem, but he set forth principles vitally important to Christian giving in general.

For various reasons, many members of the church at Jerusalem were in a state of material distress, if not destitution. Acts 11:27–30 tells us of a widespread famine, apparently especially severe in Jerusalem, and of how the Christians at Antioch "each according to his ability, determined to send relief to the brethren dwelling in Judea." This relief was then taken to Jerusalem by Paul and Barnabas.

At the time Paul was writing to the Corinthians, the plight of the Jerusalem Christians was again—or perhaps *still*— difficult. A year before this epistle was written, the church at Corinth had begun to take up a collection for these needy brethren, but the project had been put aside, perhaps because of the turmoil in the Corinthian assembly. Now, with the spiritual obstacles removed, Paul felt it was time to continue and complete the offering.

## THE SUPREME MOTIVE

Throughout chapters 8 and 9 the apostle stressed the decisiveness of the spiritual factor in Christian giving. Such self-abnegation must be an expression of *grace*, a word which appears repeatedly in these chapters. In fundraising campaigns we often see appeals made to our selfishness ("in return for your gift we will send to you. . ."), or to their vanity ("your name as a donor will appear on. . ."). Humor is used to cajole or dark hints used to threaten. None of these devices would have been considered by Paul. The supreme motive for giving is a loving, grateful response to God for His unspeakable gift, ". . . our Lord Jesus Christ, [who] though He was rich, yet for [our] sakes He became poor, that [we] through His poverty might become rich" (8:9).

## THE MACEDONIAN MODEL

To illustrate giving as a grace, Paul cited the example of the Macedonian churches, which included the Philippians, Thessalonians, and Bereans. Living in a region harshly treated by Rome, these people suffered severe economic hardship. But so motivated by grace were the Macedonian Christians in love and liberality that they have become the classic model for the church of the ideal manner of Christian giving.

In verse 2 Paul employed several contrasts which emphasized the beauty of the grace of God in these Macedonian believers. He wrote of their "great trial of affliction" and "their deep poverty" in the same sentence as "the abundance of their joy" and "the riches of their liberality." Afflictions were their lot, both because they were of Macedonia and because, in a deeper sense, they were of Christ. But the spirit with which they endured their affliction reveals to us the splendid quality of their faith. This "abundance of joy" is not, we must acknowledge, a typical description of afflicted Christians. Usually the song of the soul, if not silenced, is at least muted. The countenance may reflect patient hope, but seldom that rapturous attitude of the Macedonians.

Their joy is all the more remarkable in view of the fact that besides the severe test of affliction, they faced the perennial problem of poverty—which is, in the minds of many people, the ultimate calamity. Furthermore, theirs was not a poverty defined by theorists never exposed to personal indigence; the apostle, who himself lived in constant hunger and thirst, poorly clothed and homeless, speaks of their condition as "*deep poverty.*" If ever a company of Christians might have excused themselves from giving to others, these were they. If the apostle had told us that they had expressed regret over their present situation and promised, when conditions improved, to share in the collection, we would understand and sympathize. Instead we must be amazed at what Paul said: Out of their extreme poverty, the Macedonians responded to the needs of the Jerusalem Christians with overflowing liberality.

Nothing is said of how *much* they gave—it could not have been a large amount—but *how* they gave is the subject of Paul's admiration. It is axiomatic that the test of Christian giving—perhaps *all* giving, whether Christian or not—is not how much is given but how much is left *after* giving. The truest giving depends not on full purses but on full hearts.

One wonders how many of these lovely saints gave of their grain and then went home with abounding joy to an empty, or nearly-empty, cupboard; how many of them retrieved old garments once put aside, to wear in place of better ones sent to Jerusalem. What beautiful Christians they were! Are we anything like them?

## PATTERN FOR GIVING

In 1 Corinthians 16:2, the apostle gave instructions concerning the collection for the saints: "On the first day of the week let each one of you lay something aside, storing up *as he may prosper*. . . ." The Macedonian churches, despite their afflictions and poverty, joyously disregarded this reasonable formula for proportionate giving. "According to their ability, yes, and *beyond* their ability, they were freely willing" to help those in need. The fund was not, for them, an unpleasant and unwelcome test of their benevolence; it was an opportunity to allow the grace of God to be manifested in their gifts.

This fund was not being raised for the purpose of building a church or college, employing a ministerial staff, sending missionaries, supporting a Sunday school, or conducting evangelistic services. As strictly a collection for the needy Christians in Judea, it is an example of only one kind of giving. Nevertheless, what Paul said concerning it, and the Macedonian response, underline some basic and essential factors for all Christian giving.

There are degrees and kinds of liberality which may be judged in the light of that Macedonian response. First, let's look at the people most condemned by such a comparison: those who give less than their means allow, even to the point of giving nothing. Such a level of Christianity, if it *be* Christianity, defies understanding. Being a Christian means loving God and our Savior, Christ; how can we refuse to give for His glory? That we may give without loving is undeniable, but that we may love without giving is impossible. The validity of a faith which accepts God's gifts of grace, but refuses to share His gifts with others, is suspect.

Others give "according to their ability," but their poor attitude robs them of the joy which should accompany their gifts. Their offering is placed in the plate as a routine religious duty, with little or no thought of the One who laid down His life for our salvation. Or they may give for the sake of appearance, rather than for the love of Christ. John Mott said long ago, "The world asks, 'How *much* does he give?' Christ asks,

'Why does he give?' " Another temptation of those who give according to their ability is their inclination to "keep books" of their giving. Their concern for recognition and appreciation from the church, and even from God, can take the form of insistence upon specifying the purpose of their gifts or upon the right to supervise the use of them.

There are even those who give beyond their ability, but not for proper reasons. They give for effect, for the admiration their apparent sacrifice elicits, or, sometimes, to outdo someone else.

From such inadequacy we turn to the Macedonian-style givers! Paul clearly indicated that they gave *sacrificially,* "beyond their ability or means," more than anyone could reasonably require or expect of them. One form of generosity, of course, is more reckless than generous, springing out of improvidence rather than benevolence. The Macedonians, however, were obviously not guilty of this fault since their condition was one of deep poverty; their giving called for selfless sacrifice.

They also gave *willingly:* ". . . freely willing, imploring us with much urgency that we would receive the gift. . . ." This language suggests that Paul, aware of their destitution, told them that nothing would be expected of them, and that they, in turn, implored—actually begged—him to accept the gift. How many times have we heard such an entreaty in the church?

Finally, and most importantly, the gift of the Macedonians was precious because it was offered *worshipfully.* They "first gave themselves to the Lord, and then to us by the will of God." Motivated as they were by humane, compassionate feelings, their giving was, first and primarily, to God.

We have mentioned those who deposit their offerings in a routine, mechanical manner, with scarcely a thought of gratitude or partnership with God. Troubled about this tendency when I was a pastor, I urged my congregation always to place their offerings in the plate with a silent, personal prayer, such as this: "Dear Lord, accept my gift with My love and gratitude for Your love and goodness to me." Many people told me that this practice brought new, blessed meaning to a part of the service too often barren of worship.

Let us learn to worship through giving. Assuredly we want to give generously, willingly, and wisely, but above all let us make our gifts a conscious, loving act of worship.

# 20

## CHRIST, THE SUPREME GIFT

*2 Cor. 8:6–15*
  **6** So we urged Titus, that as he had begun, so he would also complete this grace in you as well. **7** But as you abound in everything—in faith, in speech, in knowledge, in all diligence, and in your love for us—see that you abound in this grace also. **8** I speak not by commandment, but by occasion of the diligence of others and to prove the sincerity of your love. **9** For you know the grace of our Lord Jesus Christ, that though He was rich, yet for your sakes He became poor, that you through His poverty might become rich. **10** And in this I give my advice: It is to your advantage not only to be doing what you began and were desiring to do a year ago. **11** but now also complete the doing of it; that as there was a readiness to desire it, so there also may be a completion out of what you have. **12** For if there is first a willing mind, it is accepted according to what one has, and not according to what he does not have. **13** For I do not mean that others should be eased and you burdened, **14** but by an equality, that now at this time your abundance may supply their lack, that their abundance also may supply your lack—that there may be equality. **15** As it is written, "He who gathered much had nothing left over, and he who gathered little had no lack."

We have previously noted that the fund for relief of the needy Jerusalem saints had been started but suspended (it is widely believed) because of the Corinthian turmoil. Numerous unhappy events result from ruptured fellowship. One of the most insidious consequences is its paralytic effect upon the positive, progressive, and beneficial activities of the church. Projects which deserve attention, and are essentially if not primarily the reason for the church's existence, are subordinated to the dissension.

## THE VENTURE OF CHRISTIAN COMPASSION

Surely the strife among the Corinthian believers, as well as their lapse of confidence in and submission to Paul, displaced their concern for the truly important purposes of the church. One of these concerns was the collection for the indigent saints. Once the problems at Corinth were resolved, Paul exhorted the Christians there to turn their attention to their previous project.

A somewhat oblique compliment to Titus was included here. His usefulness to Paul, and to the church at large, was vital but nowhere greater, perhaps, than in his ability to guide the Corinthians in paths of restoration and recovery of spiritual soundness. The effect of his teaching should be contrasted to that of demagogues and malcontents who usually falsely profess to have the best interests of the people in mind, but who frequently *cause* problems rather than solve them. Instead of such agitators, we need the help of those in whom the Spirit of Christ dwells and works for peace and reconciliation.

Also evident in the recognition of Titus' gift was Paul's humility and modesty. The apostle did not feel that *he* had to lead the collection or be credited with it. He had no desire for personal recognition; his concern was the spiritual health and usefulness of the church.

## GIVING CERTIFIED BY LOVE

Take note also of Paul's positive and tactful language. "You abound," he wrote, "in faith, in speech, in knowledge, in all diligence, and in your love for us—see that you abound in this grace [or, this gracious work] also." The Corinthians, just as we, needed to be reminded that every person and every church has strengths in some areas which may be neutralized by weaknesses in others. Whatever gift or virtue one may possess, its effectiveness is compromised unless it is accompanied by love and concern for others.

The apostle made clear that he was not imposing a command: "I speak not by commandment . . ." (v. 8); ". . . I give my advice . . ." (v. 10). He cited the example of the Macedonians to encourage them, but the decision was left to the Corinthians. Liberality and love cannot be produced on command, or by legal requirement. One can be forced to give, but not forced to *want* to give. Paul could not require them to love, but he did obviously feel that his call to them to share in the fund was a test of the sincerity of their love.

## THE SUPREME GIVER

The ninth verse of this chapter is one of the momentous ones of the epistle. Whatever other example, incentive, or inspiration we have for liberality and compassion, Christ is our supreme example. He was rich beyond our comprehension but accepted—*embraced*—poverty for our sakes, that we might become rich in the true treasures, those which are eternal.

Many terms and figures are used to praise and exalt our Savior. One must still wonder, though, if their sum expresses enough of His *generosity*. Equal with God the Father, He did not cling to that equality, but "emptied Himself . . . humbled Himself" (Phil. 2:7,8), surrendered His riches to live without a place to lay His head, in a world which resented and crucified Him! Although Paul discussed grace elsewhere in the chapter (vv. 1,6,7), here he taught that Christ gave in grace, and that His Spirit in believers inspires and incites them to do the same. The Macedonian example was noble and gracious, but His was beyond any human comparison.

## THE BLESSINGS OF GENEROSITY

A neglected truth in this passage appears in verse 10: "It is to your advantage . . ." to complete the collection. Not only did the needy saints benefit—so did the Corinthians. There is a very real sense in which Christian giving—*true* Christian giving, in the name and Spirit of Christ—brings us into a deeper fellowship with the Father, who gave His Son, and with the Son, who gave Himself. This kind of giving is part of God's process of making us like Himself.

A dear lady of very limited means wrote a check to her church, the amount of which was much larger than her bank balance. The pastor gently asked her why she did this. She answered, "Oh, I want to show my feelings, my good intentions!" She had what is called in verse 12 "a willing mind," but she overlooked the other condition: ". . . it is accepted according to *what one has,* and not according to what he does not have." God knows our means and honors our giving according to those means.

The apostle also reminded the Corinthians that, as they shared of their abundance, they could confidently trust in the Savior's promise, should the day come when they were in need, "Give, and it will be given to you . . ." (Luke 6:38). Those to whom they were now to give might, on another occasion, be the ones who would come to *their* assistance. That aid would then be given in a spirit of reciprocity, but more importantly, in grace, love, and compassion.

# 21

## MESSENGERS
## WHO MEASURE UP

*2 Cor. 8:16–24*

**16** But thanks be to God who put the same earnest care into the heart of Titus for you. **17** For he not only accepted the exhortation, but being more diligent, he has gone to you of his own accord. **18** And we have sent with him the brother whose praise is in the gospel throughout all the churches, **19** and not only that, but who was also chosen by the churches to travel with us with this gift, which is administered by us to the glory of the same Lord and declaration of your ready mind, **20** avoiding this: that anyone should blame us in this lavish gift which is administered by us— **21** providing for honorable things, not only in the sight of the Lord, but also in the sight of men. **22** And we have sent with them our brother whom we have often proved diligent in many things, but now much more diligent, because of the great confidence which we have in you. **23** If anyone inquires about Titus, he is my partner and fellow worker concerning you. Or if our brethren are inquired about, they are messengers of the churches, the glory of Christ. **24** Therefore show to them, and before the churches, the proof of your love and of our boasting on your behalf.

Sometimes those in Christian service take a proprietary attitude toward their congregation. They seem to feel, if not to say, "These are *my* converts, my trophies, for Christ. I do not want others to tamper with them or to interfere with the progress I am seeking to produce in their lives." Although Paul was the founder of the church at Corinth, having spent eighteen months of arduous and effective ministry there, he did not perceive himself as the only one suitable to lead the Corinthians in the ways of God. His concern for them has been often and lovingly manifested in this epistle, but, at the end of the eighth chapter, he welcomed and thanked God for the interest and love shown by Titus.

In verse 6, Paul disclosed his urging of Titus to lead the Corinthians in the completion of the fund for Jerusalem and Judea. In the passage under consideration, we learn that Titus not only *accepted* this assignment but *welcomed* the opportunity to go to Corinth, and had left of his own accord. Only secondarily was the trip's purpose to raise money though; Titus intended to lead the Corinthians in a mission of grace, so that they might develop—and abound in—the grace of liberality.

## NEEDFUL URGING

Those who object to, and even resent, exhortations to give monetarily for spiritual and benevolent purposes should realize that such urging is for their benefit. Similarly, admonitions to pray, to feed the soul on the Scriptures, and to foster other spiritual means of growth are beneficial, if obeyed. Once again let us consider verse 10, "It is to *your advantage*. . . ." Possibly in no other area do Christians show their inconsistency more than in the matter of giving. We may endorse, even hallow, the *idea*, but so often fail in the *practice*.

Titus was accompanied by several select persons about whom Paul made some intriguing comments. The first was referred to as simply a "brother" who was highly esteemed by the churches for his preaching of the gospel and was chosen by the churches to be a part of the team. Who was he? There has been much speculation, but no convincing evidence concerning his identity. *Who* he was is moot, uncertain; *what* he was is clear. He was a gifted, honorable, respected brother in Christ. Surely that is identification enough! To be *eminent* may be pleasant, but to be *excellent* is better!

## THE IMPORTANCE OF INTEGRITY

Verses 18–21 manifest Paul's consciousness of possible suspicions being raised in Corinth. Thus, he stressed the integrity and reputation of the unnamed brother as a witness to the manner in which the fund was to be collected and administered.

Those who raise money for spiritual and benevolent purposes may sometimes be tempted to use such funds for personal advantage; whether they do so or not, they are *certain* to be suspected of it. Sadly, some cause for suspicion has been created by an occasional fundraiser's irresponsible use of money entrusted to him for the work of the Lord. Paul knew his own mind and had no question of his own integrity, but he wanted men, as well as God, to know that his actions were above reproach.

The apostle mentioned another "brother," in verse 22, who was to join the team. He was commended as one known for his diligence and devotion, which had been proven "in many things." He accepted this new assignment with an even greater enthusiasm, being impressed with the Corinthians' attitude. Then Paul spoke of Titus, in the event that any question should be raised concerning him: ". . . he is my partner and fellow worker concerning you," explained the apostle, implying that Titus's feelings toward the Corinthians were the same as Paul's. Finally, a sentence was added about the two unnamed brethren; they are "messengers of the churches [apostles, in the sense of being sent ones]" and "the glory of Christ," a phrase which must mean that their lives were lived to His glory. Paul introduced this team to the Corinthians, urging the church to receive them in Christian love and to measure up to the commendations he had expressed concerning them.

Throughout the passage it is evident that Paul recognized the importance of personal integrity and prudence, as well as of public confidence. Those who have been "put in trust with the gospel" must always be aware that they are responsible not only for what they *are* but, insofar as they are able to determine, what they *seem* to be. On the other hand, those who are careful about appearances but careless about conscience are a menace to the cause of Christ. Even if their consciences are clear, being injudicious about appearances can damage influence and neutralize the effect of the gospel.

# 22

## GOD WILL PROVIDE

*2 Cor. 9:1–9*

**1** Now concerning the ministering to the saints, it is superfluous for me to write to you; **2** for I know your willingness, about which I boast of you to the Macedonians, that Achaia was ready a year ago; and your zeal has stirred up the majority. **3** Yet I have sent the brethren, lest our boasting of you should be in vain in this respect, that, as I said, you may be ready; **4** lest perhaps if some Macedonians come with me and find you unprepared, we (not to mention you!) should be ashamed in this same confident boasting. **5** Therefore I thought it necessary to exhort the brethren to go to you ahead of time, and prepare your bountiful gift beforehand, which you had previously pledged, that it may be ready as a matter of bounty and not as covetousness. **6** But this I say: He who sows sparingly will also reap sparingly, and he who sows bountifully will also reap bountifully. **7** So let each one give as he purposes in his heart, not grudgingly or of necessity; for God loves a cheerful giver. **8** And God is able to make all grace abound toward you, that you, always having all sufficiency in all things, may abound to every good work. **9** As it is written: "He has dispersed abroad, He has given to the poor; His righteousness remains forever."

Paul had spoken in glowing terms to the Macedonians about the liberality of the Corinthians in contributing to the fund "a year ago," or, as some scholars believe the wording should be, "last year." It would have been embarrassing to him and to the Corinthians—and disillusioning to the Macedonian representatives—to discover that such boasting was not supported by facts. Here at the opening of the ninth chapter we learn that the apostle was confident that the Corinthians would be ready with their contribution, but he wisely sent Titus and the two other brethren in advance just to make sure.

The words "boast" and "boasting" in these verses should be
understood as proper and proud satisfaction on the part of the
apostle rather than carnal, vain bragging (see Chapter 3).

## REAPING FOLLOWS SOWING

Human generosity must rise above the human tendency to
fear that giving to others—and even to God—will cause a
depletion in resources and a condition of need. The extreme
effect of such fear is the hoarding of money which should be
spent on personal concerns. We may well suppose that some
citizens of Corinth, caught in this fear, were uneasy about
giving, at least about giving substantially. Thus, the apostle
taught that giving is sowing, and that reaping *follows* sowing.
To be sure, Christian giving is above all an expression of love
and worship of our Lord, but it is also a means of sowing seed for
the benefit of ourselves as well as others. "The liberal soul shall
be made fat [or shall be enriched] . . ." reads Proverbs 11:25.
Stinginess shrivels the soul, but liberality of hand and heart
brings richness of life.

## THE PROPER ATTITUDE FOR GIVING

The apostle emphasized the *spirit* in which we are to give as
well as the *measure* we should give. He wanted everyone to
realize that money given unwillingly, or because of a feeling of
obligation, cannot foster growth in our souls. One of the
hazards we face as we consider church budgets, quotas, and
goals is that we may give "grudgingly," feeling that church
leaders are imposing an unfair burden on us, and "of necessity,"
rather than cheerfully sowing financial seed to produce spiritual
bounties.

## TRUST AND OBEY

A Christian businessman related an incident to me once

which became a spiritual summit in his life. Having pledged a substantial amount for the cause of Christ, with his wife's full consent he doubled the amount, then tripled it. They thought it would be necessary to borrow money to pay their pledge, but the success of his business made this unnecessary. The loveliest part of the story is what this adventure in Christian giving fostered in their spiritual experience. Twenty years afterward, as they told the story, their faces were aglow with spiritual joy! They learned personally the meaning of verse 8: "God is able to make all grace abound toward you, that you, always having all sufficiency in all things, may abound to every good work."

God will *always* provide what is needed for His purposes. The life of faith may be said to be simply a life committed to that fact. Consider the beautiful demonstration of Abraham, as he prepared to offer his son, Isaac, on the altar. When Isaac, not knowing that he was the designated sacrifice, asked his father, ". . . where is the lamb for a burnt offering?" (Gen. 22:7), Abraham answered, ". . . my son, God will provide Himself a lamb for a burnt offering . . ." (22:8). Hebrews 11:19 tells us that Abraham was counting on God to raise up Isaac from the dead. And "God will provide for Himself" what is needed in and through us, as we trust and obey Him.

# 23

## EXPRESSING OUR THANKS

2 Cor. 9:10–15

10 Now may He who supplies seed to the sower, and bread for food, supply and multiply the seed you have sown and increase the fruits of your righteousness, 11 being enriched in everything for all liberality, which causes thanksgiving through us to God. 12 For the administration of this service not only supplies the needs of the saints, but is also abounding by many thanksgivings to God, 13 while, through the proof of this ministry, they glorify God for the obedience of your confession to the gospel of Christ, and for your liberal sharing with them and all men, 14 and by their prayer for you, who long for you because of the exceeding grace of God in you. 15 Thanks be to God for His unspeakable gift!

The last six verses of chapter 9 conclude Paul's comments concerning the fund for the needy saints. Verses 10 and 11 are commonly considered to be a supplication to God by Paul, that the seed the Corinthians have sown (in providing for those in need) may be supplied and multiplied; that the fruits of their righteousness, or generosity, may be increased; and that they may be enriched in everything as a result of their generosity. A different rendering of these verses, however, also has strong support among scholars. The verbs in the Greek are future indicative, so it is likely that what is being said is that God *will* supply, *will* multiply, *will* increase and enrich, a translation which makes certain the conditional "may" in verse 10.

### THE SUPREME BENEFIT

How beautiful that Christlike compassion and generosity toward those in need, as stated in verses 12–14, not only relieve distress but commend to the afflicted the grace of God, thus inspiring thanksgiving. The supreme benefit of all benevo-lence, as well as of all worship, is that God be glorified. Thus the fund, offered in His name and Spirit, would have produced praise to Him on the part of those who received it. At the same time it would have endeared the Corinthians to their bene-ficiaries, whose subsequent prayers for their generous Gentile brethren would have been offered frequently, gratefully, and lovingly.

The passage, the chapter, and the section close with an expression of praise: "Thanks be to God for His unspeakable gift!" Behind and above all Christian giving is that supreme, inexpressible, inestimable gift of God's Son for our salvation. Paul's writings often carry us to the heights of wonder and praise as they tell of God's grace in Christ. Some passages are so filled with ecstatic gratitude that we cannot help but see the hand of the Divine Author, the Holy Spirit, writing through the apostle. But all he could say, even with the Spirit guiding his heart and hand, could not express what this supreme gift meant to him, and to us. Human language can portray only the outline of His divine character, the faint footprints of His life, the mere foam from the sea of His mercies, and just a hint of His immeasurable might.

Our kindergarten minds never can assess fully the worth of this supreme gift of God to us, but we can comprehend, however dimly, that it was a gift of love—the deepest and holiest love. Our sin and our estrangement from God can then be perceived as a rejection, not of His condemnation of us, but of His unfathomable *love*; placed in such a context, unbelief grows increasingly shameful and abhorrent.

This unspeakable gift includes and encompasses other gifts—in some ways it may be said to include *all* others. James understood that "Every good gift and every perfect gift is from above . . ." (James 1:17). All we possess seems better, *is* better, when we possess God's supreme gift. We cherish nature's beauty more as Christ opens our eyes to it. We appreciate human personalities more, as we see what fellowship in Christ is. And we love the Bible more, as we find in it God's marvelous gift.

One should always thank the giver of a gift—surely *such* a gift—but how do we express our thanks to God? First, we give ourselves and all we have to Him, recognizing that we are not our own but His, purchased with His blood. ". . . those who live should no longer live for themselves, but for Him who died for them and rose again" (2 Cor. 5:15). Moreover, we are to express our thanks by sharing the gift with others. Every believer should feel responsible for sharing the gospel with others in the same measure he has received it.

## THE MULTIPLICATION PROCESS

Let us review some of the basic facts of Christian giving taught or suggested in this section: (1) As our Savior said, "It *is* more blessed to give than to receive." (2) We are not poorer for our self-denial and sacrifice, but richer, for our gifts open to us the riches of God. (3) Our lack of liberality issues from a fear for our own future and security, thus rejecting the promise of God to care for us and to bless our giving. (4) The problem is not one of economics when we withhold our possessions from God; it is one of withholding love from God and His cause and from men's souls. (5) Our giving pleases God and enriches our own lives; done in the Spirit of Christ, it also inspires thanksgiving and praise to God on the part of others.

# 24

## GENTLE STRENGTH AND QUIET POWER

*2 Cor. 10:1–6*

**1** Now I, Paul, myself am pleading with you by the meekness and gentleness of Christ—who in presence am lowly among you, but being absent am bold toward you. **2** But I beg you that when I am present I may not be bold with that confidence by which I intend to be bold against some, who think of us as if we walked according to the flesh. **3** For though we walk in the flesh, we do not war according to the flesh. **4** For the weapons of our warfare are not carnal but mighty through God for pulling down strongholds, **5** casting down arguments and every high thing that exalts itself against the knowledge of God, bringing every thought into captivity to the obedience of Christ, **6** and being ready to punish all disobedience when your obedience is fulfilled.

Much has been written and said about the abrupt change of tone evident in the tenth chapter, which introduces the final segment of this epistle. Paul was affectionate and commendatory in chapters 8 and 9, concluding with a rapturous expression of praise for God's wondrous gift to man. Then, in chapters 10–13, he turned to a defense of his person, his character, and, primarily, his ministry. Several explanations have been posited for this switch in tone, among them the theory that Paul felt compelled to express himself in terms of appreciation and gratitude for the loyal, unwavering members of the Corinthian church. That out of the way, however, he could then speak frankly about the opposition, even slander, which had been expressed about him and his ministry.

Another hypothesis is that these chapters are part of the "stern" or "severe" letter Paul is said to have written (and to

which he supposedly refers in the passages 2:3,9, and 7:8), and
that the rest of that letter has been lost.

## THE VOICE OF AUTHORITY

The position taken in these studies is that no valid reason
exists to consider this passage a random, or accidental, attach-
ment to Second Corinthians. As stated earlier, Paul was not
organizing a treatise; he was expressing his concern about the
state of the Corinthian church. No structural purpose existed
to prevent Paul from dealing with matters as they were brought
to his mind under the Holy Spirit's guidance.

The switch in tone we find in these first verses of chapter 10 is
not, however, from deep affection to caustic criticism. Given
the nature of the opposition, sarcastic and untruthful, the
apostle expressed his grievance in a contrasting tone of temper-
ance and pacificity. He began with an appeal to them, "by the
meekness and gentleness of Christ," that, in person, he would
not be forced to deal with the rebellious faction in a harsh
manner. Having been accused of timidity when present and
boldness only when safely distant, he did not wish to disprove
their charges by asserting himself. Spiritual, not carnal,
weapons were Paul's armament as he tried to imitate his Lord's
spirit of meekness, that self-forgetting concern for the glory of
God and the benefit of others. Shakespeare termed meekness
"calm, dishonorable, vile submission," which is perhaps defini-
tively correct in the common usage of his time and ours, but far
from the biblical implications of the word. A Christian's
meekness is strength, but gentle strength; power, but quiet
power; humility, not insipid ("I am nothing") but profound
("Christ is everything").

## SPIRITUAL WARFARE

Paul's description of "the weapons of our warfare" is crucially important in our understanding of the walk and work of the Christian life. We are not to resort to carnal methods of opposition in seeking to serve our Lord. Our dependence should instead be upon the same weapons as He employed— those invincible forces of "love, joy, peace, long-suffering, kindness, goodness, faithfulness, gentleness [and] self control" (Gal. 5:22). The natural mind rejects such weapons, preferring to resort to violent means which breed further strife; but our spiritual weapons are invincible in the service of God, defeating all that opposes His will and knowledge. With them every thought is brought "into captivity to the obedience of Christ."

It should also be remembered that Paul was defending his message and his apostleship. He took note of personal aspersions against himself, but his main concern was that the spiritual blessings and benefits which came to the Corinthians through his ministry should not be dissipated through the negative efforts of a small group.

An important prerequisite for effective spiritual warfare is mentioned in verse 6, where Paul wrote of the disobedient being punished "when your [the church's] obedience is fulfilled." He implied here what he stated explicitly in numerous other places. The church is a body whose members are joined first to Christ as head and then to each other. It is unthinkable that such a body should be divided between the obedient and disobedient. When a majority is indifferent to the delinquency of some members, the health of the body is compromised. Paul called for those who were not delinquent to become fully submitted to Christ, every thought captive to Him. After such submission, the disobedient could be identified by contrast to be then dealt with according to spiritual principles.

These first six verses of chapter 10 should be read carefully by every group of Christians undergoing times of schism. "For the weapons of our warfare *are not carnal,*" wrote Paul; resorting to such methods compounds problems and grieves our Lord. The church can never be healed by one member of the body claiming priority over another, just as our physical bodies cannot be healed by isolating an injured part.

# 25

## AUTHORITY IN THE CHURCH

2 Cor. 10:7–11

**7** Do you look at things according to the outward appearance? If anyone is convinced in himself that he is Christ's, let him consider this again in himself, that just as he is Christ's, even so we are Christ's. **8** For even if I should boast somewhat more about our authority, which the Lord has given us for edification and not for your destruction, I shall not be ashamed— **9** lest I seem to terrify you by letters. **10** "For his letters," they say, "are weighty and powerful, but his bodily presence is weak, and his speech contemptible." **11** · Let such a person consider this, that what we are in word by letters when we are absent, such we will also be in deed when we are present.

The sentence opening this middle section of chapter 10 has been the subject of debate. The words can be understood either as a question or a statement, but the majority of scholars seem to consider them an affirmation. In either case, Paul was challenging the Corinthians to study the true facts, rather than mere outward appearances.

## OUTWARD APPEARANCES ARE NOT EVERYTHING

This admonition involves a persistent problem of the church. The fundamental factors determining the nature of truth, properly the supreme concern of the church, have often been considered with indifference. The lesser, sometimes even unworthy, matters and people are accepted and honored instead.

A similar failing of spiritual sight must have occurred in the Corinthian church. Those who opposed Paul should have been

recognized easily as false teachers and self-important pre-
tenders, bent upon depriving the churches of the liberty of
Christ and putting them under the bondage of the law. Their
message was clothed in such guile, though, with such claims of
authority and orthodoxy, that many Corinthian believers suc-
cumbed to their wiles.

One of the claims they made, we gather, was that they had
known Jesus in the flesh and thus spoke with far greater
authority than Paul. To this Paul responded, "If anyone is
convinced in himself that he is Christ's . . . even so we are [I
am] Christ's." Paul did not know Jesus before his conversion,
but on the Damascus road he had a personal encounter with
Him which far transcended that professed by the false teachers.

## IN DEFENSE OF APOSTOLIC AUTHORITY

The apostle acknowledged that he might be boasting too
much about his authority (v.8), but he was not ashamed of
doing so. He placed a supreme value on that authority, for it
was bestowed upon and entrusted to him for the edification of
the church. With a fierce faithfulness manifested in his words
to the Philippians, he accepted his commission to preach, but
more importantly, to defend the gospel. Such faith reminds us
by contrast of the man Paul once was: ". . . a Hebrew of the
Hebrews; concerning the law, a Pharisee; concerning zeal,
persecuting the church . . ." (Phil. 3:5,6). As a bigoted and
bitter Pharisee he had been fiercely anti-church and anti-
Christ, and bent on the destruction of the gospel. This epistle
also manifests a zeal and sanctified fierceness, but it is an energy
determined to protect the church, to contend for the faith, to
oppose at whatever cost the mutilation of the gospel of grace.
What an exhilarating change was wrought in the heart and life
of the one-time Saul of Tarsus! Once he had carried letters of
authority to bring believers to Jerusalem in chains; later he sent
letters to Corinth, "weighty and powerful" letters, in which he

declared that those who have found liberty in Christ are not to be "entangled again with a yoke of bondage" (Gal. 5:1).

His adversaries acknowledged the effectiveness and force of his letters but spoke with scorn of his physical appearance and speech. The phrase, "his bodily presence is weak," may be an insult concerning Paul's *person* rather than a slur on his appearance, but it seems more likely that it was meant *both* ways. Paul's opening comment in this passage, concerning judging by outward appearance, was probably made with this calumny in mind. In all candor, it may be that Paul's speech was not of a quality to be admired by the Greeks. Theirs was a culture which produced some of the great orators of history. Paul would not have pretended to excel as a public speaker, nor would even his friends credit him with skill in elocution. Elsewhere he declared that his purpose was not to declare the testimony of God with excellency of speech or of man's wisdom, "but in demonstration of the Spirit and of power, that your faith should not be in the wisdom of men but in the power of God" (1 Cor. 2:4,5).

Whoever spoke so disparagingly of Paul's bodily presence and speech was told in verse 11 to expect Paul to be as firm and forceful in person as his letters had been. It was not his wish to be severe but, if the health of the church was at stake, Paul would do what he must, in accordance with his apostolic authority.

The church of our day needs to recover respect for authority in the church. Neither doctrine nor policy is to be determined by mere human decisions. Instead we should endeavor to discover what the divine Word expresses and accept the authority of those whom God has called to implement the commands of that Word.

# 26

## GOD'S APPROVAL,
## THE CROWNING TRIBUTE

*2 Cor. 10:12–18*

**12** For we dare not make ourselves of the number, or compare ourselves with some, who commend themselves. But they, measuring themselves by themselves, and comparing themselves among themselves, are not wise. **13** But we will not boast beyond measure, but within the limits of the sphere which God appointed us—a sphere reaching even to you. **14** For we are not extending ourselves beyond our sphere, as though not reaching you, for we came even to you with the gospel of Christ; **15** not boasting of things beyond measure, that is, in other men's labors, but having hope, that as your faith is increased, we shall be greatly enlarged by you in our sphere, **16** to preach the gospel in the regions beyond you, and not to boast in another man's sphere of accomplishment. **17** But "He who glories, let him glory in the Lord." **18** For not he who commends himself is approved, but whom the Lord commends.

As he sought to correct the thinking of the Corinthians and diminish the damage done by the interlopers who sought to overthrow his influence, Paul did not—dared not—enter into the spirit of self-praise which these false apostles manifested.

As they praised themselves, these men found pleasure in comparing their personal gifts with those of their unworthy associates—a gratifying experience, since they could see little in the others to make them conscious of their own shabby character. Placing ourselves on a scale of character with any other individuals blinds us to what we are, as well as to what we can and should be.

## PAUL'S DESCRIPTION OF HIMSELF

Paul's eyes were upon his Lord. He wanted, above all else, to know Him, to be conformed to His will, to receive His approval. Anything which would hinder him in his quest of that prize he considered rubbish, not worthy of a moment's attention.

The apostle might have been tempted to answer the boasting of his adversaries with boasting of his own. He was aware that such a tactic might go beyond legitimate limits, however, and was on guard against that possibility. He realized that his ministry in Corinth, as everywhere, was all of grace. Satisfaction and joy were his in what he had been enabled to do (which is what he means by "boast"), but he never lost sight of the fact that he served by God's appointment and achieved by His enablement.

Even if he did not boast as did his adversaries, Paul wanted his authority made clear. He was saying in essence, "Our coming to you was by divine assignment, not—as the intruders' was—a presumptuous venture unauthorized and unapproved by God. We came to you, not arrogantly boasting of ourselves, but with the gospel. And we were the *first* to come to you with that gospel" (see v. 14).

His detractors had come to claim the credit for what others had achieved, while Paul's aim was always "to preach the gospel, not where Christ was [or, had been] named, lest I should build on another man's foundation." His hope was that the faith of the Corinthians would grow strong and stable so that his ministry *to* them would become a ministry *through* them. Passive receptivity would then be transformed into active aggression, with Paul, in service of Christ.

As the Corinthians achieved a more mature and steadfast spiritual state, Paul planned to turn his attention to other fields, to "the regions beyond" them, while depending upon them to share his vision and burden. Such is the ideal process of spiritual blossoming and growing in grace and faith until fit for service, recognizing our place of service, finding God's plan for us, and growing strong by helping to bear the burden of the work. As we take those steps, it is vital to remember Paul's admonishment against taking the credit for work already done by others. Each Christian has his place, whether planting, watering, or reaping, "but God [gives] the increase" (1 Cor. 3:6). Spiritual maturity and integrity will cause us to respect and honor others for their labors, while giving praise to God for the increase.

The difference in spiritual strength between Paul and the false teachers is manifestly evident in their varying approaches to the Corinthian situation. Paul was steadfast, confident, knowing he was obeying divine orders and would be given divine resources. His adversaries were pushing, intruding, arrogantly pretending to be what they were not and claiming credit for what they had not done, seeking praise from others and heaping it on themselves. Their actions, if recognized for what they were, condemned themselves.

## CREDIBLE BOASTING

This talk of boasting—and practice of it—was unpleasant for the apostle, even though he felt it was necessary. Paul did not seek glory; his prayer was always: "God forbid that I should glory except in the cross of our Lord Jesus Christ . . ." (Gal. 6:14). Another wording of the same message is his abridgement of Jeremiah 9:24: "He who glories, let him glory in the Lord." Though rejecting the claims of the false apostles that they had accomplished what he had actually done, Paul would neither credit to himself what had, in reality, been accomplished only by God's enabling grace.

The passage closes with a landmark verse. The factious teachers had made much of letters of credentials, to which Paul's response had been "You are our epistle [letter] . . .

written not with ink but by the Spirit of the living God . . . "
(3:2,3). He dealt with their boasting and their seeking to
establish themselves in the esteem of the people similarly: "Not
he who commends himself is approved, but whom the Lord
commends." To be commended by the Lord is the ultimate,
crowning tribute, whether men approve or not. However we
may seem to succeed, however men may applaud, if we do not
have *His* approval, we have failed.

# 27

## IN DEFENSE OF THE TRUTH

*2 Cor. 11:1–9*

**1** O that you would bear with me in a little folly—and indeed you do bear with me. **2** For I am jealous for you with godly jealousy. For I have betrothed you to one husband, that I may present you as a chaste virgin to Christ. **3** But I fear, lest somehow, as the serpent deceived Eve by his craftiness, so your minds may be corrupted from the simplicity that is in Christ. **4** For if he who comes preaches another Jesus whom we have not preached, or if you receive a different spirit which you have not received, or a different gospel which you have not accepted, you may well put up with it. **5** For I consider that I am not a bit behind the most eminent apostles. **6** And though I am untrained in speech, yet I am not in knowledge. But we have been thoroughly made manifest among you in all things. **7** Have I committed sin in abasing myself that you might be exalted, because I have preached the gospel of God to you free of charge? **8** I robbed other churches, taking wages from them to minister to you. **9** And when I was present with you, and in need, I was a burden to no one, for what was lacking to me the brethren who came from Macedonia supplied. And in all things I have kept myself from being burdensome to you, and so I will keep myself.

In his concern for the Corinthians, the apostle resorted to what he felt was, or may be considered to be, foolishness. What he was about to say here at the opening of chapter 11 was so much out of character for him that he felt awkward saying it. The circumstances forced him to continue, though, and he asked the Corinthians to bear with him and hear him out. He was sure that they would give him that courtesy.

## DIVINE JEALOUSY

Reading Paul's admission of being jealous is unsettling until
we recognize the nature and reason for it. We are accustomed to
thinking of this emotion as Talmadge described it, "a diabolical
sin which sets one half the world against the other." Jealousy
has been called the shadow of other people's success. It is the
fear of or apprehension of another's superiority, and as such is
poisonous and destructive.

What we are calling a divine jealousy is of another order.
God speaks of Himself as "a jealous God," meaning that He will
accept no rival for His place, that He is solicitous for our welfare,
and that He demands our full loyalty. Likewise, Paul's jealousy
was divine or godly, springing out of his distress over the
wavering Corinthians, not out of personal pique. He wanted to
present this church to Christ as a pure bride, un-corrupted
"from the simplicity that is in Christ." Fear of a defection that
would be a triumph for Satan—and a tragic blow to the church
at large—made Paul jealous. Whatever the Corinthians' feelings toward him, he could not bear to see them turn from
Christ.

## BEWARE OF FALSE TEACHERS

Furthermore, listening to the false teachers would not help
prevent this defection, for Paul made clear that these men were
not introducing new and different aspects of the blessed gospel
he had preached. They were presenting *another* Jesus, in a
*different* spirit, and preaching a *different* gospel. And the
Corinthians' acceptance of this other Jesus, this satanic spirit,
and this corrupted gospel brought anguish to the apostle.

Some of the Corinthians were blinded by false claims of
superiority over Paul and thus deceived into listening to this
false preaching. We know how preposterously arrogant this
position was since Paul led both the spiritual and intellectual

march of the church into its historical witness to the world. Paul did not make so grand a statement, but only modestly stated that he was not in the least inferior to "the most eminent apostles."

Some writers believe this expression refers sarcastically to the false teachers. Another opinion, and the position of this author, is that Paul had in mind the true apostles. He acknowledged, as he did elsewhere, that though he was not smooth-tongued he had a gift more vital than glibness. To him God imparted a special revelation and gave a unique commission— to preach Christ to the Gentiles. His message, as he told the Galatians, was not given to him by human instruction but by divine revelation. One does not have to be a skilled orator to make the truth plain.

## CONSCIENTIOUS VINDICATION

Another contrast of Paul's method to that of the false apostles is that they apparently required payment for their services. Paul had taken wages from a church so beleaguered financially that he felt he was robbing them, in order to avoid being a burden to the Corinthians. The destitute Macedonian Christians had contributed to his support so that the Corinthians might have no reason to consider Paul's ministry and presence a financial liability.

Apparently this conscientiousness was interpreted by the Corinthians as an admission of inferiority—that Paul did not feel worthy of being paid by those to whom he ministered— rather than as a demonstration of unselfish concern for them. Paul's clarification of his motives implied the question, Could they not see the difference between the methods of himself and of his adversaries? In any case, he would continue to minister without charge. His God and his integrity were of greater importance to him than the superficial opinions of men.

As we read Second Corinthians and see, both implicitly and

explicitly, the petty and sometimes contemptible attitude of the people to whom Paul wrote, we are led to marvel at the long-suffering, patient Christian attitude of the apostle. Many ministers would agree that if treated similarly to Paul, they would certainly resign. The apostle remained valiant: He was so caught up with the eternal significance of what he was doing, so abandoned to the call of God, so committed to the ministry which God had entrusted to him, that he counted everything else "as rubbish" that he might "finish his course and testify to the gospel of the grace of God."

# 28

## FALSE APOSTLES AND
## TRUE APOSTLES

*2 Cor. 11:10–22*

**10** As the truth of Christ is in me, no one shall stop me from this boasting in the regions of Achaia. **11** Why? Because I do not love you? God knows! **12** But what I do, I also will continue to do, that I may cut off the opportunity from those who desire an opportunity that in what they boast they also may be regarded just as we are. **13** For such are false apostles, deceitful workers, transforming themselves into apostles of Christ. **14** And no wonder! For Satan himself transforms himself into an angel of light. **15** Therefore it is no great thing if his ministers also transform themselves into ministers of righteousness whose end will be according to their works. **16** I say again, let no one think me a fool. If otherwise, at least receive me as a fool, that I also may boast a little. **17** What I speak, I speak not according to the Lord, but as it were, foolishly, in this confidence of boasting. **18** Seeing that many boast according to the flesh, I also will boast. **19** For you put up with fools gladly, seeing you yourselves are wise! **20** For you put up with it if one brings you into bondage, if one devours you, if one takes from you, if one exalts himself, if one strikes you on the face. **21** To our shame, I say that we were too weak for that! But in whatever anyone is bold—I speak foolishly—I am bold also. **22** Are they Hebrews? So am I. Are they Israelites? So am I. Are they the seed of Abraham? So am I.

With solemn phrasing Paul declared that, as the truth of Christ was in him, he would not allow anything or anyone to keep him from glorying in his independence of support from the Corinthians. Those who feel his opponents accused Paul of a cold and loveless attitude suggest that his refusal to accept support from

the Corinthians was evidence of that disposition. But Paul was
not motivated by a lack of love; rather his purpose here was to
expose the false apostles as "deceitful workers, transforming [or
disguising] themselves as apostles of Christ."

## DECEITFULNESS EXPOSED

His restraint, evident throughout the first third of chapter
11, was now put aside, to be replaced by a withering indictment
of the false teachers. Their deceit, both in motives and actions,
needed to be exposed, while at the same time Paul had to be
careful to give them no advantage. Pay was again an issue here,
for if the false prophets took no money, it was to deceive the
people into thinking they were serving in an altruistic, unselfish way. Thus, if Paul had taken money, the false teachers
could have twisted the facts to discredit him and to commend
themselves. Paul, though he did serve *willingly* without com-
pensation, was also *wise* in doing so.

That such men could get away with masquerading as apostles
should come as no surprise, for Satan can persuade men that he
is an angel of light. This is an oblique but very evident charge
by Paul that the false apostles were satanically motivated. Their
iniquitous actions were to be expected and their punishment
would be as severe as the disgusting degree of their hypocrisy.

## RELUCTANT BOASTING

Next, in verse 16, Paul turned again to the topic he found so
awkward to discuss. He felt he had to meet the opposition with
the same weapons they were using. Disclaiming any divine
authority at this point, he says (in paraphrase): "I speak not
according to the Lord (that is, by His assignment) but in foolish
boasting. That should be no problem for you. In your supposed
wisdom, you put up with fools gladly. You can be brought into
bondage. You can be consumed. You can be plundered. You
can be physically assaulted by those who come exalting them-

selves and abasing you. You accept their claims and you submit
to their arrogance. Perhaps I should be ashamed to say it, but I
could not treat you that way. Let me state my case, foolish
though it may be thus to commend myself. I shall speak
boldly."

## THE TEST

Paul built his case with the series of questions found in verses
22–23. He asked concerning the false teachers, "Are they
Hebrews?" (Do they speak the Hebrew language in Aramaic
form, free from Greek contamination?) "Are they Israelites?"
(Are they genuinely of the true covenant people?) "Are they of
the seed of Abraham, his direct physical descendents?" To each
of these questions Paul answered, "So am I." The rhetorical
nature of the questions indicates that the false ones had established their identity as being Hebrews, Israelites, and of Abraham's seed. Possibly they had used Paul's description of himself as an apostle to the Gentiles to raise doubts about his
Hebrew lineage.

We shall find, in verse 23, that Paul next turned from
Hebrew language, covenant prestige, and ancestral
privilege—which are of no advantage so far as being Christian
is concerned—and asked, "Are they ministers of Christ?" In
that question is the challenge: "If they are, let us compare their
service with mine." The record of Paul's service in terms of
hardship and steadfastness when perceived in the light of truth
was something the false teachers could not combat. Paul's
heroic character and commitment to Christ, even as only
partially divulged in this chapter, were matchless.

# 29

## A SUFFERING SERVANT

*2 Cor. 11:23–33*

**23** Are they ministers of Christ?—I speak as a fool—I am more: in labors more abundant, in stripes above measure, in prisons more frequently, in deaths often. **24** From the Jews five times I received forty stripes minus one. **25** Three times I was beaten with rods, once I was stoned, three times I was shipwrecked, a night and a day I have been in the deep; **26** in journeys often, in perils of waters, in perils of robbers, in perils by my own countrymen, in perils by the Gentiles, in perils in the city, in perils in the wilderness, in perils in the sea, in perils among false brethren; **27** in weariness and toil, in sleeplessness often, in hunger and thirst, in fastings often, in cold and nakedness— **28** besides the other things, what comes upon me daily: my anxiety for all the churches. **29** Who is weak, and I am not weak? Who is made to stumble, and I do not burn with indignation? **30** If I must boast, I will boast in the things which concern my infirmity. **31** The God and Father of our Lord Jesus Christ, who is blessed forever, knows that I am not lying. **32** In Damascus the governor, under Aretas the king, was guarding the city of the Damascenes with a garrison, desiring to apprehend me; **33** and I was let down in a basket through a window in the wall, and escaped his hands.

In several places in his Corinthian letters Paul alluded to his afflictions and adversities for his Lord. But here at the end of chapter 10, reluctantly he goes into detail to show to the Corinthians the falsity of the charges made against him. He did not, even under unpleasant provocation, give a full account of his sufferings; but what he wrote creates a vivid picture of what our Lord meant when He told Ananias (Acts 9:16) that Paul was to suffer "great things" for His sake.

## LABORS: TO SPEND AND BE SPENT

His "labors" were "more abundant" than those of the opposition. In 12:15 he declared his purpose to "spend and be spent" for his beloved Corinthians. His labors brought him to the point, no doubt frequently, at which this phrase aptly described him.

## BEATINGS

Beatings were a commonplace experience for the apostle who had endured "stripes above measure" (or countless beatings) by both Jews and Gentiles. In verses 24 and 25 he described receiving from the Jews forty stripes "minus one." (Forty was the maximum number of stripes allowed by the Jewish Law; the practice was to stop at thirty-nine to avoid a violation.) "Three times" he received a beating "with rods," which was the Roman method, administered to him illegally since he was a Roman citizen (see Acts 22:24–29).

## IMPRISONMENTS

Imprisonments were also a frequent ordeal for Paul. At the time of this epistle only one confinement in prison had been recorded, and that in Acts 16, but we know that Acts does not purport to be a full account of Paul's experiences.

## NEAR DEATH

"In deaths often" obviously means that Paul was frequently near death but spared from it by divine intervention. A touching example of such affliction is found in Acts 14:19, which recounts Paul's being stoned by a multitude at the instigation of "Jews from Antioch and Iconium." He refers to this time of near-death (indeed, he was believed to be dead) in verse 25.

## SHIPWRECKS

Paul mentioned three shipwrecks, though only one is recorded (Acts 27) and that one took place at a later date than the writing of this epistle. Thus, before his life was over, he experienced at least four such ordeals and spent, at some time, "a night and a day in the deep."

## DANGEROUS TRAVELS

During his "journeys often" he was in constant peril. Travel in those days was much more difficult and dangerous even for the average man than in modern times. Paul was imperiled by "waters" (raging rivers) and by "robbers" (brigands who would kill their victims without hesitation). His political and religious enemies who had sworn to kill him only compounded the situation. Even his "own countrymen" would have killed him as readily as the robbers, perhaps more readily, and the Gentiles were equally hostile. In danger from the Jews because he preached salvation to the Gentiles, Paul was also considered an enemy by the Gentiles because he was a Jew. Neither city nor wilderness offered a haven; and even worse than a blatant attack on his person was the danger from those who claimed to be brethren but who sought to destroy his reputation and to subvert the churches he had hewn out of paganism.

Paul's review of his sufferings concludes with a brief mention in verse 27 of various kinds of affliction, such as sleeplessness and hunger, and then leads into his final concern: "besides the other things, . . . my anxiety for all the churches" (v. 28).

## PAUL'S PASTORAL HEART

Verse 29 gives us a glimpse into the pastoral heart of the apostle. Whenever one of his flock was weakened in faith, Paul shared the pain and shame of his weakness. When one was "made to stumble," Paul "[burned] with indignation." His depth of caring for the Corinthians, the basis of both of his epistles to them, was particularly manifest in the final section of this second letter (chs. 10–13) and in this verse.

Chapter 12, in the opinion of some, should begin at verse 30. The basis for this position is that Paul said here what he would repeat several times in the next chapter: ". . . I boast in the things which concern my infirmity." It was a continuing wonder to him that God could take one such as he deemed himself to be, full of infirmities (recall his description of himself in 7:5—"Outside were conflicts, inside were fears"), and make him such an extraordinary instrument in fulfilling the divine purpose.

In whichever "chapter" the verse may belong, the point made is of great importance. In verse 31 Paul solemnly called God to witness to the truth of his account of his sufferings and to the purpose of it. He did not describe his hardships and adversity in order to glorify himself but rather to restate his credentials to the Corinthians, as well as to emphasize the difference between his own apostolic love and labor and that of the false apostles.

The chapter closes with Paul seeming to recall another incident typical of his precarious way of life. He recalled how he escaped the governor of Damascus by being lowered to the ground in a basket through a window. Paul's use of the account here is not random, however; the story illustrates the indignity and humiliation, as well as the danger, which Paul often experienced as he served his Lord.

# 30

## THE STRENGTH OF WEAKNESS

*2 Cor. 12:1–10*

**1** It is doubtless not profitable for me to boast. I will come to visions and revelations of the Lord: **2** I know a man in Christ who fourteen years ago—whether in the body I do not know, or whether out of the body I do not know, God knows—such a one was caught up to the third heaven. **3** And I know such a man—whether in the body or out of the body I do not know, God knows— **4** how he was caught up into Paradise and heard inexpressible words, which it is not lawful for a man to utter. **5** Of such a one I will boast; yet of myself I will not boast, except in my infirmities. **6** For though I might desire to boast, I will not be a fool; for I will speak the truth. But now I forbear, lest anyone should think of me above what he sees me to be or what he hears from me. **7** And lest I be exalted above measure by the abundance of the revelations, a thorn in the flesh was given to me, a messenger of Satan to buffet me, lest I be exalted above measure. **8** For this thing I pleaded with the Lord three times that it might depart from me. **9** And He said to me, "My grace is sufficient for you, for My strength is made perfect in weakness." Therefore most gladly I will rather boast in my infirmities, that the power of Christ may rest upon me. **10** Therefore I take pleasure in infirmities, in reproaches, in needs, in persecutions, in distresses, for Christ's sake. For when I am weak, then I am strong.

Again we find Paul at the beginning of chapter 12 expressing his aversion to boasting, saying that it is unprofitable as well as unpleasant and unseemly. He found it necessary, though, to emphasize his visions and revelations (perhaps the false apostles had claimed to have transcendental, mystical experiences.)

## PAUL'S RAPTUROUS EXPERIENCE

Support for his claim would have been easy. Indeed, the apostle's very conversion was accompanied by such an experience. At another time the man of Macedonia appeared to him in a vision (Acts 16:9). In Corinth the Lord spoke to him in a vision, assuring him of divine help and preservation (Acts 18:9). These and other such visions and revelations might have been described by Paul here, but he turned instead to one not recorded or mentioned elsewhere. It is clear that Paul was relating his own experience, but his distaste for boasting caused him to speak of himself in the third person: "I know a man in Christ . . . such a one was caught up to the third heaven. . . ."

Much has been written speculating about where Paul was fourteen years before this writing, whether he was in the body or was transported only in the spirit (he didn't know, himself—how could we?), and what is meant by "caught up to the third heaven." Another issue is whether he was caught up twice, once to the third heaven and again to Paradise, and whether these two places are identical.

Such speculations, while they are interesting, deal only with what is incidental and subordinate to the marvelous nature and purpose of this rapturous and momentous event. What was the purpose? It was surely, in part at least, that Paul might receive the revelations of divine truth and design which were needed by him for his singular apostolic assignment. Paul knew this had nothing to do with his being venerated. Thus he said, "Of *such* a one will I boast; yet of myself I will not boast, except in my infirmities [or weakness]." He praised the "man in Christ" knowing absolutely that in his flesh "nothing good dwells" (Rom. 7:18).

## THE THORN IN THE FLESH

Still, there was the possibility that Paul might be tempted to boast of this experience, but he realized that to do so would be foolish and would tend to exalt him above measure. This possibility was also *divinely* recognized and, lest he should be unduly honored by himself or others, he was given "a thorn in the flesh . . . a messenger of Satan to buffet" him. The question, What was that thorn in the flesh? has been extensively examined. Firm and dogmatic opinions abound, usually in support of personal and particular theological positions taken by the writers and speakers, thus overlooking the more basic and beneficial truth which Paul learned from it. My opinion is that it was a physical ordeal—"in the flesh," "a messenger of Satan to buffet me"—initiated by Satan and permitted by God for His servant's benefit.

The thorn (some use the word "stake") in his flesh was neither pleasant nor welcome to Paul. He pleaded with the Lord "three times," not for the grace to endure it but that it might be taken away. Paul's prayers could not bring deliverance because God knew *His apostle needed the discipline of the thorn.* Moreover, He provided Paul with *something better,* as is always the case when the Lord does not answer our prayers as we wish Him to do. Paul was given a divine bestowment of grace, a gift of faith for *every* circumstance—a far greater gift than merely deliverance from one trial.

Paul took comfort, as we do, in God's promise: "My grace is sufficient for you. . . ." Only God can direct and form our lives in the best possible way. Every life needs certain pressures and problems which reveal our dependence on divine grace. For God to end such trials would be to deprive us of the privilege of claiming that grace, thus leading us to become self-sufficient rather than to depend upon His sufficiency. Moreover, the grace he gave Paul was more than enough to endure the trial, thus making him stronger than he would have been without it.

God continues: ". . . for My strength is made perfect in weakness" or, as W. J. Conybeare and J. S. Howson so beautifully put it, "has its full development in weakness."* It is not the weakness of ignorance, or of unbelief, or of self-sufficiency, but of entire dependence upon God, which brings strength. Therefore Paul could boast of the infirmities which made possible and actual the power of Christ upon him. He took pleasure in the very things which were naturally offensive and oppressive, because they became the means by which God's power was made manifest.

---

*The Life and Epistles of St. Paul (Grand Rapids, Mich.: Eerdmans, 1949), p. 506.

# 31

## THE SIGNS OF HONORABLE APOSTLESHIP

*2 Cor. 12:11–21*

**11** I have become a fool in boasting; you have compelled me. For I ought to have been commended by you, for in nothing was I behind the most eminent apostles, though I am nothing. **12** Truly the signs of an apostle were accomplished among you with all perseverance, in signs and wonders and mighty deeds. **13** For what is it in which you were inferior to other churches, except that I myself was not burdensome to you? Forgive me this wrong! **14** Now the third time I am ready to come to you. And I will not be burdensome to you; for I do not seek yours, but you. For the children ought not to lay up for the parents, but the parents for the children. **15** And I will very gladly spend and be spent for you; though the more abundantly I love you, the less I am loved. **16** But be that as it may, I did not burden you. Nevertheless, being crafty, I caught you with guile! **17** Did I take advantage of you by any of those whom I sent to you? **18** I urged Titus, and sent our brother with him. Did Titus take advantage of you? Did we not walk in the same spirit? Did we not walk in the same steps? **19** Again, do you think that we excuse ourselves to you? We speak before God in Christ. But we do all things, beloved, for your edification. **20** For I fear lest, when I come, I shall not find you such as I wish, and that I shall be found by you such as you do not wish; lest there be contentions, jealousies, outbursts of wrath, selfish ambitions, backbitings, whisperings, conceits, tumults; **21** and lest, when I come again, my God will humble me among you, and I shall mourn for many who have sinned before and have not repented of the uncleanness, fornication, and licentiousness which they have committed.

Throughout this epistle we have seen Paul's personal and very human distress over the need to answer the charges of the false apostles and to make his defense to the very ones who should have been his staunch supporters. They should have defended and commended him, rather than permitting him to feel so foolish in defense of himself and his apostleship.

## TRUE GLORYING

Again Paul wrote that he was not inferior to "the most eminent apostles" (by which he was referring either sarcastically to the false or factually to the true apostles; opinions differ). At the same time he acknowledged that he was "nothing," of himself. His call, his labors, his faithfulness, his sufferings—all were of grace, all possible by the enabling energy of God. This is a crucial recognition necessary for everyone who seeks to minister in Christ's name. We tend to glory in our gifts rather than in the Giver, without whom we are nothing. Or, on the other hand, we despair because we have so few gifts, forgetting the fact that God's strength can be mightily demonstrated even through our weakness.

Paul, through God's enabling power, formed a truly apostolic ministry in the Corinthian church. Sinners had been converted—the greatest of miracles—as well as other "wonders and mighty deeds." All this Paul accomplished in spite of the hindrances and difficulties he endured among them. Patiently and persistently, divinely strengthened, he had fulfilled his apostolic mission among the Corinthians.

## THE APOSTOLIC SPIRIT

Paul answered a criticism, unrecorded here, that he had not given the Corinthians the measure of affection he had shown to other churches. He indicated that because he didn't accept support from them they were resentful. Having already explained his reasons for this (11:7–12), he exclaimed in irony if not in exasperation, "Forgive me this wrong!" His large mind and heart were annoyed at this infantile pettiness.

Paul had already been in Corinth twice. He had ministered there eighteen months and had founded the church on his first sojourn. The second visit apparently followed his first epistle and was an unpleasant, painful ordeal for him. Now, in this letter, he wrote of his plans to come again, still with the purpose of giving, not receiving, and of serving, not being served, "for I do not seek yours, but you." Whatever the "signs and wonders and mighty deeds" were which marked the apostolic *ministry*, they were not greater than the apostolic *spirit* evident in these words. Whatever else Paul had said, in distress, in vexation or reproach, the cause is here: He was concerned about *them*. He had no desire for their wealth; he was supremely absorbed with their spiritual health and stability.

We see in verse 15 that Paul affirmed his purpose once again to do whatever possible for the Corinthians' benefit, whether or not his affection and dedication were appreciated and returned. The wording here is actually stronger than what has been rendered: "I will most gladly spend and be *utterly* spent *for your souls.*" This is a moving and revealing picture of Paul's pastoral and paternal feelings for these wavering people. Paul used the figure of a father and his children to state that it was not their place to provide for him in a material way.

## DEALING WITH SLANDER

Repeatedly Paul had to deal with slander. Here it is evident that his enemies charged him with refusing material support from the Corinthians merely for effect, while furtively appropriating a considerable portion of the fund for Jerusalem for himself. The apostle brushed this malicious slander aside by citing the proven fact of his own integrity, as well as that of Titus and the "brother" who accompanied him. These men

were highly esteemed and trusted, as is stated in chapter
8:18,22. Paul was strengthened against such maliciousness by a
strong, clear conscience, which kept his soul in sunlight even
in the dark, stormy times.

Moreover, though the apostle acknowledged his responsibility to answer the charges against him—and though he reasoned
with, appealed to, and rebuked his accusers and those who gave
them credibility—he declared in verse 19 that it was to God
that he was supremely, ultimately answerable. His long rebuttal
is a defense of himself and his apostleship, but even more
essentially a defense of the church against the false apostles.

We see in verses 20 and 21 that Paul expressed his dread of
coming to Corinth and finding the church infected and pol-
luted with ugly attitudes and practices of the flesh. He expressed himself with restraint but his deep concern is evident.
His goal was to present the Corinthian church to Christ as a
chaste bride. The prospect of finding them in a state of carnality
was appalling to him.

# 32

# DISCIPLINE AND AUTHORITY
# IN THE CHURCH

*2 Cor. 13:1–14*

1 This will be the third time I am coming to you. "In the mouth of two or three witnesses every word shall be established." 2 I have told you before, and foretell as if I were present the second time, and now being absent I write to those who have sinned before, and to all the rest, that if I come again I will not spare, 3 since you seek a proof of Christ speaking in me, who is not weak toward you, but mighty in you. 4 For though He was crucified in weakness, yet He lives by the power of God. For we also are weak in Him, but we shall live with Him by the power of God toward you. 5 Examine yourselves, whether you are in the faith. Prove yourselves. Do you not know yourselves that Jesus Christ is in you, unless you are disqualified? 6 But I trust that you will know that we are not disqualified. 7 Now I pray to God that you do no evil, not that we should appear approved, but that you should do what is honorable, though we may seem disqualified. 8 For we can do nothing against the truth, but for the truth. 9 For we are glad when we are weak and you are strong. And this also we pray, that you may be made complete. 10 Therefore I write these things being absent, lest being present I should use sharpness, according to the authority which the Lord has given me for edification and not for destruction. 11 Finally, brethren, farewell. Become complete. Be of good comfort, be of one mind, live in peace; and the God of love and peace will be with you. 12 Greet one another with a holy kiss. 13 All the saints greet you. 14 The grace of the Lord Jesus Christ, and the love of God, and the communion of the Holy Spirit be with you all. Amen.

Some writers suggest that Paul was not *coming* to Corinth for a third visit, but was speaking here of his third *intention* to do so. In any event, Paul made clear in this thirteenth chapter that he was coming, this time, with discipline in mind toward those polluting the life and blighting the influence of the church. He cited Deuteronomy 19:15 to indicate that such people must expect an inquest into their conduct.

## SPIRITUAL POISON MUST BE DEALT WITH

Those causing schism in Corinth had been warned previously, apparently in person. Here the apostle wrote to notify all who took part in the disruptive, even disgraceful, practices plaguing the Corinthian church that he would be relentless in dealing with this spiritual poison. Persistently and unfailingly benevolent, Paul could also be strict when unsparing measures were needed. "If I come again" is not an indication that his coming to them was in doubt. The meaning is "*when* I come again," just as in John 14:3 when Jesus said, "If I go and prepare a place for you, I will come again . . . ," or in John 16:7, "If I depart, I will send Him [the Holy Spirit] to you." The meaning is obvious in these passages.

## DIVINELY COMMISSIONED

Since the Corinthians had called for proof that Christ was speaking through him, wrote Paul, he would demonstrate without question that he was divinely commissioned as Christ's representative. Soon they would know that they were not dealing with a Christ (through His apostle) still "crucified in weakness" but One possessing "all power in heaven and in earth." Paul was coming to them, not in frail, feeble protest against their aberrations, but in the power of God. He was aware of his own human weakness but that would be no hindrance, for that weakness made possible the power of Christ in him.

## EXAMINE YOURSELVES

In anticipation of his coming and of the stern measures he was to take, the apostle admonished his readers, "Examine yourselves, whether you are in the faith." Their challenge to Paul as to whether Christ was in him was answered by his asking the same question of *them*. "Prove [test] yourselves"; "see how inconsistent you are," he called out to them (in a paraphrase): "You know that Christ is in you, unless you are disqualified [reprobates], yet you act as though I, who am your spiritual father [12:14], am disqualified [reprobate]." Paul hoped that when he arrived in Corinth the members of the church would have acknowledged his apostolic authority and dealt with their own spiritual delinquency. Of those two matters, Paul was much more concerned with their spiritual state. It is natural to appreciate recognition and approval, especially when so clearly merited; it is a demonstration of lofty, lovely Christian grace to rejoice in good even when one's personal contribution is overlooked. Truth, that divine truth which Paul proclaimed, was the supreme factor. He would do nothing, say nothing, which would diminish the impact of that truth and neutralize its blessed effect in the lives of the Corinthians.

The weakness he had endured was worthwhile if it served to strengthen them spiritually. He prayed that they might continue to grow to spiritual maturity and completeness. Then, during his visit, he could devote his efforts to a ministry of edification, rather than to discipline and denunciation. It is at times the duty of the minister of Christ to reprove and rebuke, and he fails both God and his people if he does not do so when necessary. But his joy comes in a ministry of encouragement toward spiritual responsiblity and strength.

This thirteenth chapter is a classical lesson concerning discipline and authority in the church. Paul was firm and unbending in his purpose to enforce that discipline but his words were permeated with love and tenderness. Restoration and revival, not vengeance, was his desire.

## PAUL'S BENEDICTION

The apostle concluded what must have been a difficult epistle to write with a positive, encouraging, and affectionate admonition to the Corinthians to press on to completion in Christ, to live harmoniously and peacefully together. The benediction of verse 14 has been beloved in the church for centuries. It expresses the supreme treasures of our Christian faith: the grace of Christ, the love of God, and the communion (loving fellowship and partnership) of the Holy Spirit (or, fellowship with God through the Holy Spirit).

If, as some suggest, the problems discussed in this epistle were dissipated when Paul arrived in Corinth, we can be thankful and can credit the great apostle with a deserved triumph by the grace of God.